CROCHET MANDALAS

CROCHET
MANDALAS

Marinke Slump & Anita Mundt

Dover Publications, Inc.
Mineola, New York

Bibliographical Note

Crochet Mandalas is a new work, first published by
Dover Publications, Inc., in 2015.

Cover Design: Ellen Christiansen Kraft
Interior Book Design: Christina Dieguez

International Standard Book Number

ISBN-13: 978-0-486-79135-7
ISBN-10: 0-486-79135-1

Manufactured in the United States by RR Donnelley
79135101   2015
www.doverpublications.com

Marinke,
   I hope now you have found the peace in your
heart that you searched for, and are basking barefoot
in a brilliant and beautiful light with a thousand brightly
colored flowers in your hair and a crochet hook in your hand.
   Even though you are gone, you will continue to inspire people
from the pages of this book.

                                                    Anita

Wink was an inspiring, colorful, bright, musical, and unique person.
Unfortunately she isn't here with us to celebrate this beautiful book.
Depression took her life, but she will never be forgotten. She made this
world a more colorful place and let's continue doing that for her
by being inspired by her beautiful patterns. We are so proud
of our big sister, eldest daughter, and loving girlfriend who
we love and miss very much. Heaven has gained
another angel.

CONTENTS

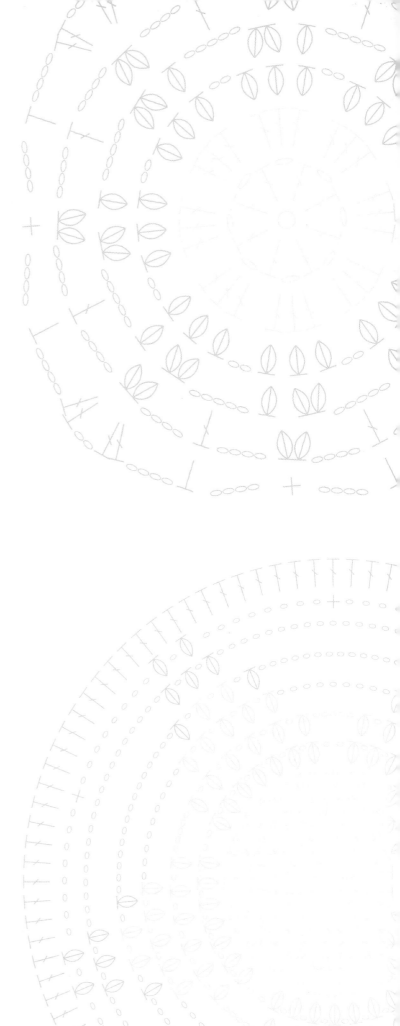

AZTEC GOLD CUSHION

Turn your home into your own personal palace with the Aztec Gold Cushion. The gold and jewel-toned color palette is inspired by ancient treasures, and the luxurious silk-blend yarn leaves it soft and shining.

AZTEC GOLD CUSHION

Designed by Marinke Slump

Sample measures approximately
15in. x 15in. (38cm x 38cm)

Materials

- Luxury Silk DK by Debbie Bliss, 50g/1.75oz
  balls, each approx. 110yd/101m
- 2 balls each in #1 Ecru (A), #14
  Buttermilk (B), #42 Spice (C)
- Crochet hook size G-6 (4mm)
- Pillow insert 13in./33cm in diameter

Stitches & Abbreviations

adjustable ring: Wrap the free end of the
yarn twice around the index and third fingers
of your left hand. With the hook and the yarn
coming from the ball, draw a loop under the
strands and into the ring. Yo and draw through
the loop to complete one chain. When the
required number of stitches have been worked
into the ring, pull on the free end of the yarn to
close the ring.

dc: double crochet

dtr: double treble crochet

ch: chain

ch-sp(s): chain space(s)

inc: increase by making 2dc into the same stitch

rep: repeat

sc: single crochet

sl st: slip stitch

sk: skip a stitch

st(s): stitch(es)

tr: treble crochet

yo: yarn over

*: work following sequence
of stitches; repeat sequence
designated number of times
more

( ): stitches between
parentheses to be
worked into the same
stitch or space

Note

Join with a sl st after
each round.

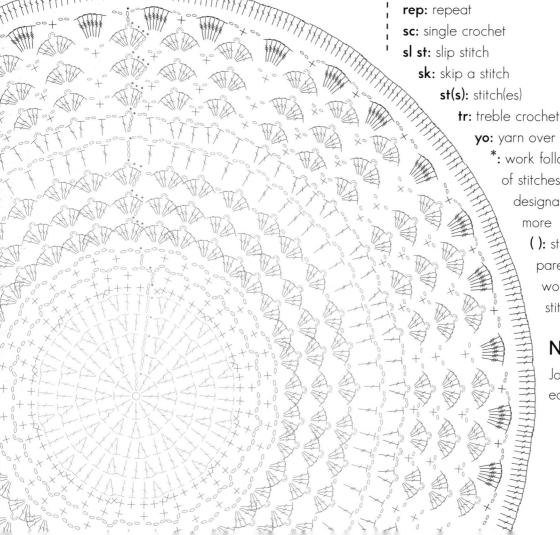

CUSHION

CUSHION SIDE (make two)

Make an adjustable ring.

Round 1
With A, work ch3 (counts as first dc), 11dc in ring—12 dc.

Round 2
ch3 (counts as dc), dc in same st, *inc; rep from * around—24dc.

Round 3
ch3 (counts as first dc), (2dc) in next st, *dc, inc, rep from * around—36dc.

Round 4
ch3 (counts as first dc), dc in next st, inc, *2dc, inc; rep from * around—48dc.

Round 5
ch3 (counts as first dc), 2dc, inc, *3dc, inc; rep from * around, changing to B in last st—60dc. Cut A.

Round 6
With B, ch2 (counts as first sc), 3sc, (2sc) in next st, *4sc, (2sc) in next st; rep from * around—72sc.

Round 7
ch5 (counts as sc, ch3), sk1, *sc, ch3, sk1; rep from * around—36 ch3-sps.

Round 8
sl st in first ch3-sp, ch5 (counts as sc, ch3), *sc in next ch3-sp, ch3; rep from * around—36 ch3-sps.

Round 9
sl st in first ch3-sp, ch3 (counts as first dc), (2dc, ch2, 3dc) in same ch3-sp, *(3dc, ch2, 3dc) in next ch3-sp; rep from * around.

Round 10
sl st in 2dc, sl st in ch2-sp, ch3 (counts as first dc), (2dc, ch2, 3dc) in same ch2-sp, *(3dc, ch2, 3dc) in next ch2-sp; rep from * around—36 ch2-sps.

Round 11
sl st in 2dc, sl st in ch2-sp, ch3 (counts as first dc), (2dc, ch2, 3dc) in same ch2-sp, ch1, *(3dc, ch2, 3dc) in next ch2-sp, ch1; rep from * around—36 ch2-sps.

Round 12
sl st in 2dc, sl st in ch2-sp, ch6 (counts as first dc, ch3), tr in ch1-sp, ch3, *dc in ch2-sp, ch3, tr in ch1-sp, ch3; rep from * around—36 tr. Fasten off.

Round 13
Join C to beginning ch3, ch5 (counts as first dc, ch2), dc in same st, ch2, dc in tr, ch2, *(dc, ch2, dc) in dc, ch2, dc tn tr, ch2; rep from * around—108 ch2-sps.

Round 14
sl st in ch2-sp, ch3 (counts as first dc), (2dc, ch2, 3dc) in same ch2-sp, ch1, sc in dc, ch1, *(3dc, ch2, 3dc) in ch2-sp, ch1, sc in dc, ch1; rep from * around—36 sc.

Round 15
sl st in 2dc, sl st in ch2-sp, ch3 (counts as first dc, (3dc, ch2, 4dc) in same ch2-sp, ch1, sc in sc, ch1, *(4dc, ch2, 4dc) in ch2-sp, ch1, sc in sc, ch1; rep from * around—36 sc.

Round 16
sl st in 3dc, sl st in ch2-sp, ch3 (counts as first dc, (3dc, ch2, 4dc in same ch2-sp, ch1, sc in sc, ch1, *(4dc, ch2, 4dc) in ch2-sp, ch1, sc in sc, ch1; rep from * around—36 sc. Fasten off.

Round 17
Join A with sl st in first ch2-sp, ch4 (counts as first sc, ch 2), (6dtr) in sc, ch2, *sc in ch2-sp, ch2, (6dtr) in sc, ch2; rep from * around—36 6dtr-groups.

Round 18
ch3 (counts as first dc), (3dc) in ch2-sp, dc in 6dtr, (3dc) in ch2-sp, *dc in sc, (3dc) in ch2-sp, dc in 6dtr, (3dc) in ch2-sp; rep from * around. Fasten off.

Finishing
Block mandalas into shape. With A, single crochet along the edge through the back loops only to join the two parts. Insert the pillow insert half way through.

BLOOMING BROOCH

Small accessories can make a big impact. Bright and vibrant, the Blooming Brooch adds personality to any outfit. Worked in DMC crochet threads, the color combinations are limitless.

BLOOMING BROOCH

Designed by Anita Mundt

Materials

- Pearl Cotton Balls #8 by DMC USA, 10g/.35oz balls, each approx. 87yd/80m (thread)
- Approx. 2g/small amounts each in #3685 Very Dark Mauve (A), #600 Very Dark Cranberry (B), #891 Dark Carnation (C), #912 Light Emerald Green (D), and #725 Topaz (E)
- Crochet hook size 12 steel (1mm)
- 1/8in/3mm approx. thick chipboard circle 2in./5cm diameter
- Scrap of linen fabric, approximately 2in./5cm diameter
- Fabric Pen
- Brooch pin
- Glue

Stitches & Abbreviations

adjustable ring: Wrap the free end of the yarn twice around the index and third fingers of your left hand. With the hook and the yarn coming from the ball, draw a loop under the strands and into the ring. Yo and draw through the loop to complete one chain. When the required number of stitches have been worked into the ring, pull on the free end of the yarn to close the ring.

ch5pc (picot using 5 chain stitches): ch5, sl st in first ch to form picot

ch-sp(s): chain space(s)

dc: double crochet

hdc: half double crochet

rep: repeat

sc: single crochet

sk: skip a stitch

sl st: slip stitch

st(s): stitch(es)

yo: yarn over

*: work following sequence of stitches; repeat sequence designated number of times more

( ): stitches between these parentheses to be worked into the same stitch or space

FRONT

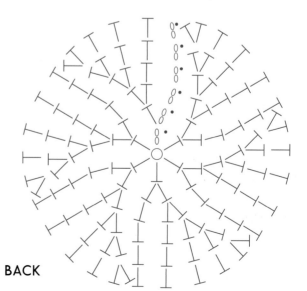

BACK

BROOCH

BROOCH FRONT

With A, make an adjustable ring.

Round 1
ch2 (counts as first sc), 5sc in ring, sl st to top of first ch2 to join—6sc.

Round 2
ch2 (counts as first sc), sc in same st, (2sc) in every stitch around, changing to B in last sc, sl st to top of first ch2 to join—12sc. Cut A.

Round 3
With B, ch1 (counts as first sl st), *ch3, sk1 sc, sl st; rep from * 5 times more, sl st to first ch1 to join—6 ch3-sps.

Round 4
*sl st in next ch-sp, ch3 (counts as first dc), (4dc) in same ch-sp, sl st in next sl st; rep from * 5 times more, sl st to top of first ch3 to join. Fasten off—6 ch3, 4dc-groups.

Round 5
Join C to first ch 3, ch2 (counts as first sc), sc in next 4dc, sc in sl st, *sc in top of ch3 from previous round, sc in next 4dc, sc in sl st; rep from * 4 times more, sl st to top of first ch2 to join—36sc. Fasten off.

Round 6
Join D to first ch2, *ch5pc, ch5, sk 5sc, sl st in next sc; rep from * 5 times more, ending with sl st to the bottom of the first ch5pc to join. Fasten off.

Round 7
Join E in loop of any ch5pc. *ch3, sl st into ch-sp, ch3, sl st in loop of ch5pc; rep from * 5 times more, sl st to first ch3 to join—12 ch3-sps.

Round 8
ch2, *4hdc in ch3-sp, hdc in next sl st; rep from * 10 times more, 4hdc in ch3-sp, sl st to top of first ch2 to join. Fasten off.

BROOCH BACK

With E, make an adjustable ring.

Round 1
ch2 (counts as first hdc), (5hdc) in ring, sl st to top of first ch2 to join—6hdc.

Round 2
ch2 (counts as first hdc), hdc in same stitch, *(2hdc) in next stitch; rep from * 4 times more, sl st to top of first ch2 to join—12hdc.

Round 3
ch2 (counts as first hdc), *(2hdc) in next stitch, hdc; rep from * 4 times more, (2hdc) in next stitch, sl st to top of first ch2 to join—18hdc.

Round 4
ch2 (counts as first hdc), hdc in next st, *(2hdc) in next stitch, 2hdc; rep from * 4 times more, (2hdc) in next stitch, sl st to top of first ch2 to join—24hdc.

Round 5
ch2 (counts as first hdc), 2hdc *(2hdc) in next stitch, 3hdc; rep from * 4 times more, (2hdc) in next stitch, sl st to top of first ch2 to join—30hdc.

Round 6
ch2 (counts as first hdc), 3hdc, *(2hdc) in next stitch, 4hdc; rep from * 4 times more, (2hdc) in next stitch, sl st to top of first ch2 to join—36hdc. Fasten off.

Finishing
Trace the chipboard circle on the fabric and cut out. Glue the fabric onto the chipboard on one side. Sandwich the chipboard between the front and back brooch pieces, with the fabric side under the front piece, and the right sides of the brooch pieces facing out. With E, slip stitch around the entire circle to join the pieces together. Glue the brooch pin to the back of the brooch.

BLOOMING BUTTON RING

Quick to make, this ring is the perfect last-minute outfit addition or handmade gift. Choose one color that embodies the wearer's personality, or mix it up and use a different color for each round.

BLOOMING BUTTON RING

Designed by Anita Mundt

Sample measures 1¹/₄in. (3cm) in diameter.

Materials

- Pearl Cotton Balls #8 by DMC USA, 10g/.35oz ball, each approx. 87yd/80m (thread)
- Approx 2g (small amount) in #600 Very Dark Cranberry or #943 Tawny
- Crochet hook size 12 steel (1mm)
- One 1in./25mm fabric covered button
- Sewing needle
- Sewing thread
- Ring shank
- Glue
- Pair of pliers

Stitches & Abbreviations

adjustable ring: Wrap the free end of the yarn twice around the index and third fingers of your left hand. With the hook and the yarn coming from the ball, draw a loop under the strands and into the ring. Yo and draw through the loop to complete one chain. When the required number of stitches have been worked into the ring, pull on the free end of the yarn to close the ring.

ch: chain

ch-sp(s): chain space(s)

dc: double crochet

rep: repeat

sl st: slip stitch

sc: single crochet

st(s): stitch(es)

yo: yarn over

*: work following sequence of stitches; repeat sequence designated number of times more

( ): stitches between parentheses to be worked into the same stitch or space

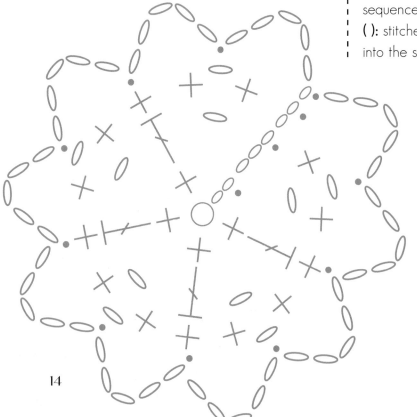

14

RING

Make an adjustable ring.

Round 1
ch2 (counts as first sc), 4sc in ring, sl st to top of first ch2 to join—5sc.

Round 2
ch4 (counts as first dc, ch1), *dc in next sc, ch1; rep from * 3 times more, sl st to top of first ch3 to join—5 ch-sps.

Round 3
ch2 (counts as first sc), *(sc, ch1, sc) in next ch-sp, sc in next dc; rep from * 3 times more, (sc, ch1, sc) in next ch-sp, sl st to top of first ch2 to join—5 ch1-sps.

Round 4
ch1 (counts as first sl st), *ch5, sl st in next ch-sp, ch5, sk next sc, sl st in next sc; rep from * 3 times more, ch5, sl st in ch-sp, ch5. sl st to top of first ch1 to join. Fasten off.

Finishing
Use the pliers to cut the shank of the button level with the edges of the button. Using sewing thread and the needle, stitch the mandala to the fabric of the button. Glue the button to the ring shank.

CELESTIAL BAREFOOT SANDALS

Combining the comfort of going barefoot with the prettiness of a sandal, the Celestial Barefoot Sandals are the best of both worlds. The delicate star motifs, worked in a luscious variegated yarn, will leave you over the moon.

CELESTIAL BAREFOOT SANDALS

Designed by Anita Mundt

Sample measures 4in. x 4in./10cm x 10 cm
without chains

Materials

- Fine Art by Rowan, 100g/3.5oz hanks,
  each approx. 437yd/100m (light fingering)
- 1 hank in #303 waxwing
- Crochet hook size B-1 or C-2 (2.5mm)

Stitches & Abbreviations

ch: chain

ch-sp(s): chain space(s)

ch5pc (picot using 5 chain stitches): ch5, sl st
in first ch to form picot

dc: double crochet

hdc: half double crochet

rep: repeat

sl st: slip stitch

sc: single crochet

st(s): stitch(es)

tr: treble crochet

*: work following sequence of stitches; repeat
sequence designated number of times more

( ): stitches between these parentheses to be
worked into the same stitch or space

BASIC

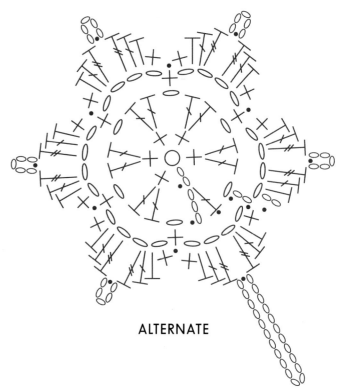

ALTERNATE

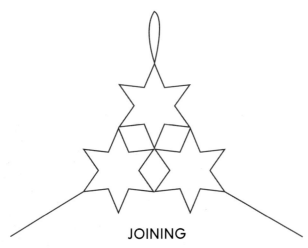

JOINING

Round 1

ch2 (counts as first sc), 5sc in ring, sl st to top of first ch2 to join—6sc.

Round 2

ch3 (counts as first dc), dc in same st, ch1, *(2dc) in next sc, ch1; rep from * 4 times more, sl st to top of first ch3 to join—6 ch1-sps.

Round 3

sl st in next dc, sl st in next ch-sp, ch6 (counts as first sc, ch4), *sc in next ch-sp, ch4; rep from * 4 times more, sl st to top of first ch2 to join—6 ch4-sps.

Round 4

sl st in next ch-sp, ch2 (counts as first sc), (hdc, dc, tr, ch5pc, tr, dc, hdc, sc) in same ch-sp, sl st in next sc, *(sc, hdc, dc, tr, ch5pc, tr, dc, hdc, sc) in ch-sp, sl st in next sc, rep from * 4 times more, ending with sl st to top of ch2 to join. Fasten off.

ALTERNATE STAR (make one for each sandal)

Work rounds 1–3 of the basic star.

Alternate Round 4

sl st in next ch-sp, ch2 (counts as first sc), (hdc, dc, tr, ch5pc, tr, dc, hdc, sc) in same ch-sp, sl st in next sc, *(sc, hdc, dc, tr, ch5pc, tr, dc, hdc, sc) in next ch-sp, sl st in next sc; rep from * 3 times more, (sc, hdc, dc, tr, ch 22, sl st in first ch, tr, dc, hdc, sc) in next ch-sp, sl st to top of ch2 to join. Fasten off.

TO MAKE THE SANDALS

Follow diagram to join, making sure 3 stars meet at the ch5 picot. Join thread to star corners (according to diagram) and ch120 for each ankle strap.

SANDALS

Join stars together following the diagram; all 3 stars meet with the ch5pc.

BASIC STAR (make two for each sandal)

ch4, join with a sl st to form ring.

DEWDROP BOWL COVER

Set the prettiest summer table for your picnic. The Dewdrop Bowl Cover does double duty, protecting your food while looking lovely. Different colored cotton threads are used to create a color gradient, and the crystal teardrop beads stabilize the cover while adding sparkle.

DEWDROP BOWL COVER

Designed by Anita Mundt

Sample measures approximately
9¹/₂in. (24cm) in diameter

Materials

- Pearl Cotton Balls #8 by DMC USA,
  10g/.35oz balls, each approx. 87yd/80m
  (thread)
- Small amount/approximately 2g in #2
  Ecru (A)
- Small amounts/approximately 1g each
  in #503 Medium Blue Green (B), and
  #943 Medium Aquamarine (C)
- Crochet hook size 12 steel (1mm)
- 12 tear drop shaped crystal beads

Stitches & Abbreviations

- - - - - - - - - - - - - - - - - - -

ch: chain

ch-sp(s): chain space(s)

dc: double crochet

pc (picot stitch): ch3, sl st in base of ch

rep: repeat

sc: single crochet

sk: skip

sl st: slip stitch

st(s): stitch(es)

*: work following sequence of stitches; repeat
sequence designated number of times more

( ): stitches between parentheses to be
worked into the same stitch or space

Note: Chart does not show beginning chains of rounds. See written instructions.

BOWL COVER

With A, ch6, sl st to first ch to form a ring.

Round 1
ch3 (counts as first dc), 11 dc in ring, sl st to top of first ch3 to join—12 dc.

Round 2
ch5 (counts as first dc, ch2), *dc, ch2; rep from * 10 times more, sl st to top of first ch3 to join—12 dc.

Round 3
sl st in next ch-sp, ch6 (counts as first sc, ch4), *sc in next ch-sp, ch4; rep from * 10 times more, sl st to top of first ch2 to join—12 ch4-sps.

Round 4
sl st in next ch-sp, ch7 (counts as first sc, ch5), *sc in next ch-sp, ch5; rep from * 10 times more, sl st to top of first ch2 to join—12 sc.

Round 5
ch5 (counts as first sc, ch3), *sc in next ch-sp, ch3, sc in next sc, ch3; rep from * 10 times more, sc in next ch-sp, ch3, sl st to top of first ch2 to join—24 sc.

Round 6
sl st in next ch-sp, ch6 (counts as first sc, ch4), *sc in next ch-sp, ch4; rep from * 22 times more, sl st to top of first ch2 to join—24 sc.

Round 7
sl st in next ch-sp, ch7 (counts as first sc, ch5), *sc in next ch-sp, ch5; rep from * 22 times more, sl st to top of first ch2 to join—24 sc.

Round 8
sl st in next ch-sp, ch8 (counts as first sc, ch6), *sc in next ch-sp, ch6; rep from * 22 times more, sl st to top of first ch2 to join—24 sc.

Round 9

sl st in next ch-sp, ch8 (counts as first sc, ch6),
*sc in next ch-sp, ch6; rep from * 22 times
more, sl st to top of first ch2 to join—24sc.

Round 10

sl st in next ch-sp, ch3 (counts as first dc), (5dc)
in same ch-sp, ch2, *6dc in next ch-sp, ch2; rep
from * 22 times more, sl st to top of first ch3 to
join—24 6dc-groups.

Round 11

sl st in 5dc, sl st in ch-sp, ch3 (counts as first dc)
5dc in same ch-sp, ch2, *(6dc) in next ch-sp,
ch2; rep from * 22 times more, sl st to top of
first ch3—24 6dc-groups. Fasten off.

Round 12

Join B in any ch-sp. ch3 (counts as first dc), 5dc
in same ch-sp, ch1, *(6dc, ch2, 6dc), in next ch-sp,
ch1; rep from * 22 times more, 6dc in next ch-sp,
ch2, sl st to top of first ch3 to join—24 ch2-sps.

Round 13

sl st into *previous* ch2-sp, ch8 (counts as first sc,
ch6), *sc in next ch1-sp, ch6, sc in next ch2-sp,
ch9, sc in next ch2-sp, ch6; rep from * 10 times
more, sc in next ch1-sp, ch6, sc in next ch2-sp,
ch9, sl st to top of first ch2 to join—12 ch9-sps.
Fasten off.

Round 14

Thread 12 beads on C. Join C in sc before any
ch9-sp, ch2 (counts as first sc), (2sc, 2hdc, 2dc,
2tr, pc (slip 1 bead into center of the picot), 2tr,
2dc, 2hdc, 2sc) in same ch-9 sp, sc in next sc,
6sc in next ch-sp, sl st in next sc, 6sc into ch-
sp, *sc in next sc, (2sc, 2hdc, 2dc, 2tr, pc (slip 1
bead into center of the picot), 2tr, 2dc, 2hdc,
2sc) in same ch-9 sp, sc in next sc, 6sc in next
ch-sp, sl st in next sc, (6sc) in next ch-sp; rep
from * 10 times more, sc in next sc, sl st to top
of first ch2 to join. Fasten off.

RAINBOW LEAVES MANDALA

The Rainbow Leaves Mandala borrows elements of traditional doilies and thoughtfully updates them for the modern crafter. The unique mix of stitch patterns and colorful yarn adds a welcome burst of color to any space.

RAINBOW LEAVES MANDALA

Designed by Marinke Slump

Sample measures approximately
17¹/₂in. (44.5cm) in diameter

Materials

- Hand spun and rainbow ombré-dyed sport or DK yarn (I used BFL), about 300yd/275m
- Crochet hook size E-4 (3.5mm)

Note

Chart does not show beginning and end of rounds. See written instructions.

Stitches & Abbreviations

adjustable ring: Wrap the free end of the yarn twice around the index and third fingers of your left hand. With the hook and the yarn coming from the ball, draw a loop under the strands and into the ring. Yo and draw through the loop to complete one chain. When the required number of stitches have been worked into the ring, pull on the free end of the yarn to close the ring.

BLO: through back loops only

FLO: through front loops only

ch: chain

ch-sp(s): chain space(s)

dc: double crochet

dtr: double treble crochet

inc: increase by making 2dc into the same stitch

rep: repeat

sc: single crochet

sk: skip a stitch

sl st: slip stitch

st(s): stitch(es)

tr: treble crochet

yo: yarn over

*: work following sequence of stitches; repeat sequence designated number of times more

( ): stitches between parentheses to be worked into the same stitch or space

[ ]: repeat sequence of stitches between brackets designated number of times

ROUNDS 1–8

MANDALA

Make an adjustable ring.

Round 1
ch7 (counts as tr, ch3) *tr, ch3; rep from * 6 times more in ring—8tr.

Round 2
sl st in ch-sp, ch3 (counts as first dc), 4dc in same ch3-sp, *(5dc) in next ch3-sp; rep from * around—40dc.

Round 3
FLO of round 2: ch2 (counts as hdc), hdc in next dc, (3tr) in next dc, 2hdc, *2hdc, (3tr) in next dc, 2hdc; rep from * around.

Round 4
BLO of round 2: ch3 (counts as dc), 6dc, inc, *7dc, inc; rep from * around—45dc.

Round 5
FLO of round 4: ch2 (counts as hdc), (3tr) in next st, hdc in next st, *hdc in next st, (3tr) in next st, hdc in next st; rep from * around.

Round 6
BLO of round 4: ch3 (counts as dc) 7dc, inc, *8dc, inc; rep from * around—50dc.

Round 7
FLO of round 6: ch2 (counts as hdc), (3tr), *hdc, (3tr); rep from * around.

Round 8
BLO of round 6: ch3 (counts as dc), 3dc, inc, *4dc, inc; rep from * around—60dc.

Round 9
ch 9 (counts as sc, ch7, sk4, sc, *ch7, sk4, sc; rep from * around—12 ch7-sps.

Round 10
sl st in ch7-sp, ch2 (counts as sc), (9sc) in same ch7-sp; *(10sc) in next ch7-sp; rep from * around—120sc.

Round 11
sl st in 2 sc, ch4 (counts as tr), 2tr, ch3, 3tr, sk2, *sk2, 3tr, ch3, 3tr, sk2; rep from * around—12 ch3-sps.

Round 12
sl st to ch3-sp, ch2 (counts as sc), (2sc, ch3, 3sc) in ch3-sp, ch3, sk3, sc between 3tr-clusters, ch3, *(3sc, ch3, 3sc) in ch3-sp, ch3, sk3, sc between 3tr-clusters, ch3; rep from * around—12 ch3-sps.

Round 13
sl st to ch3-sp, ch5 (counts as first dtr), (6dtr) in same ch-sp, ch1, dc in next ch3-sp, ch1, dc in sc, ch1, dc in next ch3-sp, ch1; *(7dtr) in ch3-sp, ch1, dc in next ch3-sp, ch1, dc in sc, ch1, dc in next ch3-sp, ch1; rep from * around—12 7tr-groups.

Round 14
sl st in next tr, ch5 (counts as dc, ch2), sk1, dc, ch2, sk1, dc, ch2, sk2, (7dtr) in middle dc, ch2, sk2, *dc in 2nd tr of group, ch2, sk1, dc, ch2, sk1, dc, ch2, sk2, (7dtr) in middle dc, ch2, sk2; rep from * around—12 7dtr-groups.

Round 15
sl st in ch-sp, ch5 (counts as sc, ch3), [sc in ch-sp, ch3] twice, *sc in center dtr of group, ch3, [sc in ch-sp, ch3] 4 times; rep from * 8 times more, sc in center dtr of group, ch3, sc in ch-sp, ch3—60 ch3-sps.

Rounds 16-17
sl st in ch-sp, ch5 (counts as sc, ch3), *sc in next ch-sp, ch3; rep from * around—60 ch3-sps.

29

Round 18

sl st in ch-sp, ch7 (counts as sc, ch 5), *sc in next ch-sp, ch5; rep from * around—60 ch5-sps.

Round 19

sl st in ch-sp, ch3 (counts as first dc) (dc, ch2, 2dc) in same ch5-sp, *(2dc, ch2, 2dc) in next ch5-sp; rep from * around—60 ch2-sps.

Round 20

sl st to ch2-sp, ch3 (counts as first dc) (6dc) in same ch2-sp, *(7dc) in next ch2-sp; rep from * around. Fasten off. Block into shape.

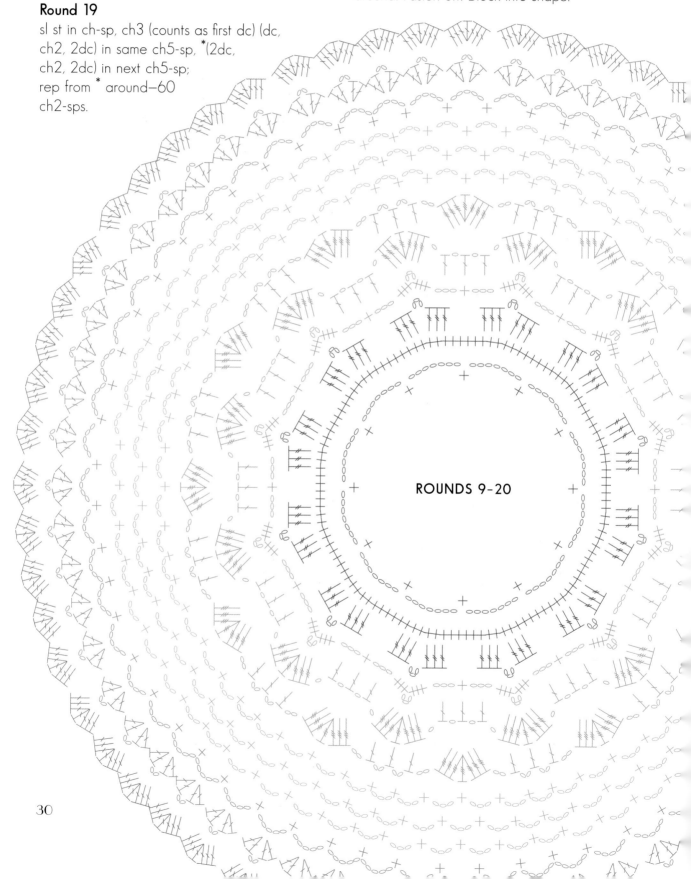

ROUNDS 9–20

EMERALD MUSE JOURNAL COVER

Personalize any plain notebook with a beautiful, colorful mandala. Worked in a linen blend, you can customize the palette with your favorite colors. Make a bunch in different hues for an inspired color-coding system.

EMERALD MUSE JOURNAL COVER

Designed by Marinke Slump

Sample measures approximately:
8in. x 8in. (20cm x 20cm)

Materials

- Panama by Rowan, 50g/1.75oz balls,
  each approx. 148yd/130m (fingering)
- 1 ball each in #301 Daisy (A), #314
  Mizzle (B), #310 Aster (C), and #309
  Lotus (D)
- Crochet hook size E-4 (3.5mm)

Stitches & Abbreviations

ch: chain

ch-sp(s): chain space(s)

dc: double crochet

rep: repeat

sk: skip a stitch

sl st: slip stitch

st(s): stitch(es)

*: work following sequence of stitches; repeat
sequence designated number of times more

( ): stitches between parentheses to be worked
into the same stitch or space

Note: Join with a sl st after each round.

JOURNAL COVER

With A, ch6, join with sl st to form ring.

Round 1

ch3 (counts as dc), dc in ring, ch2, *2dc in ring, ch2; rep from *4 times more—6 ch2-sps. Fasten off.

Round 2

Join B in first ch-sp, ch3 (counts as dc) (2dc) in same ch-sp, ch3, *(3dc) in next ch-sp, ch3; rep from * around—6 ch3-sps. Fasten off.

Round 3

Join C in first ch-sp, ch3 (counts as dc), (2dc, ch2, 3dc) in same ch-sp, *(3dc, ch2, 3dc) in next ch-sp; rep from * around—6 ch2-sps. Fasten off.

Round 4

Join A in first ch-sp, ch3 (counts as dc), (2dc, ch2, 3dc) in same ch-sp, ch1, dc between 3dc-clusters, ch1, *(3dc, ch2, 3dc) in ch-sp, ch1, dc between 3dc-clusters, ch1; rep from * around. Fasten off.

Round 5

Join B in first ch-2 sp, ch3 (counts as dc), (3dc, ch2, 4dc) in same sp, ch1, sk ch1-sp, dc in next dc, ch1, sk ch1-sp, *(4dc, ch2, 4dc) in next ch2-sp, ch1, sk ch1-sp, dc in next dc, ch1, sk ch1-sp; rep from * around. Fasten off.

Round 6

Join D in first ch2-sp, ch3 (counts as dc), (3dc, ch2, 4dc) in same sp, sk ch1-sp, (2dc, ch2, 2dc) in next dc, *(4dc, ch2, 4dc) in next ch2-sp, sk ch1-sp, (2dc, ch2, 2dc) in next dc; rep from * around. Fasten off.

Round 7

Join D in first ch2-sp, ch3 (counts as dc), 7dc in same ch2-sp, ch 1, *(8dc) in next ch2-sp, ch1; rep from * around—12 ch1-sps. Fasten off.

Finishing

Block into shape. Attach to journal with clear craft glue.

FOREST MANDALA SHRUG

The stunning central motif in the Forest Mandala Shrug turns this effortless garment into a show-stopper. The design radiates from the motif's points, with the edges ending in gentle ripples that graze the body. The vest's construction makes it suitable for all body types.

FOREST MANDALA SHRUG

Designed by Marinke Slump

Gauge: 22 rows and 30 sts = 4in. (10cm)
Sample measures 17½in. (44cm) measured across back panel and 28in. long

Materials

- Summerspun by Rowan, 50g/1.75oz balls, each approx. 131yd/120m (DK)
- 10 balls in #111 Picadilly
- Crochet hook size H-8 (5mm)

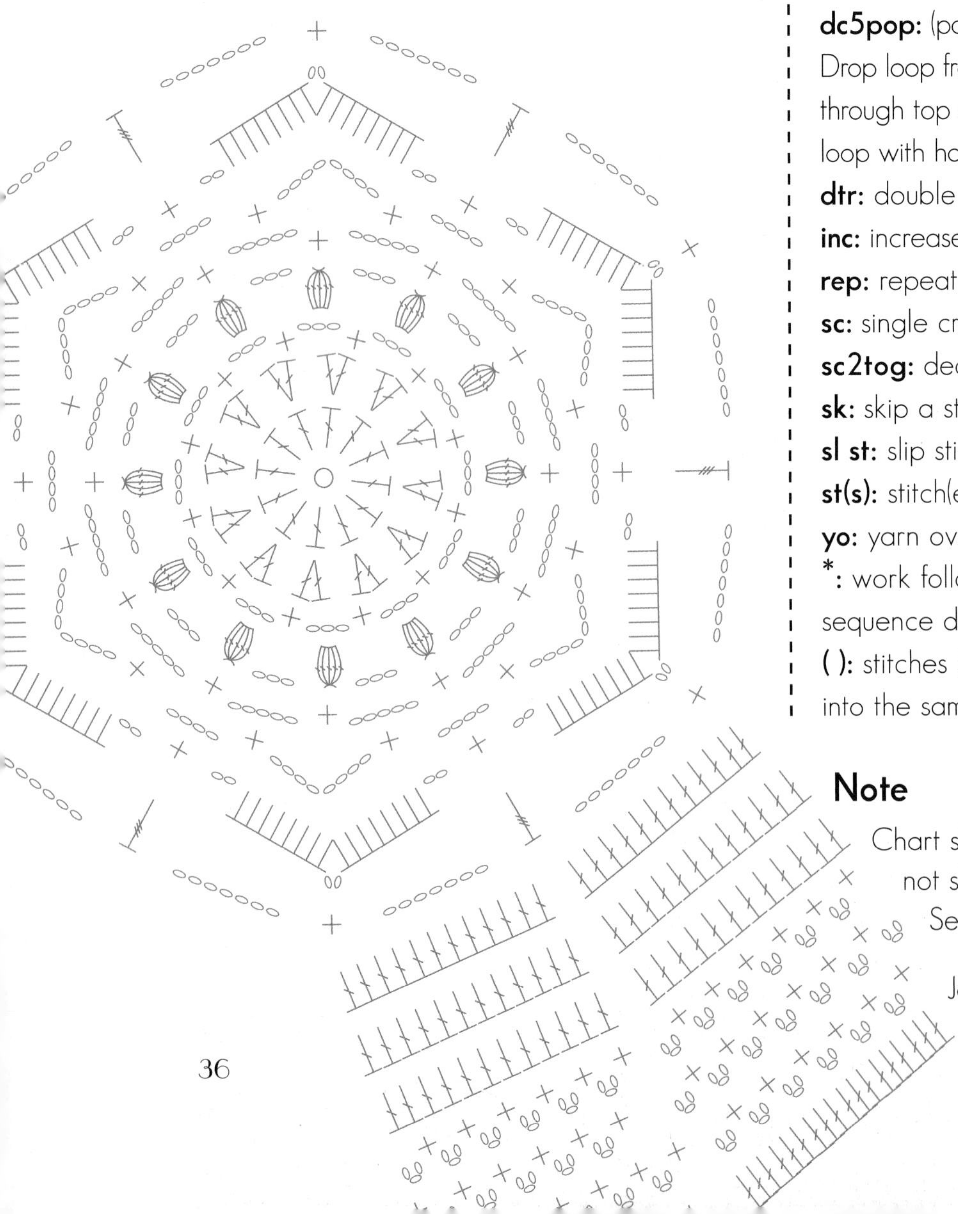

Stitches & Abbreviations

adjustable ring: Wrap the free end of the yarn twice around the index and third fingers of your left hand. With the hook and the yarn coming from the ball, draw a loop under the strands and into the ring. Yo and draw through the loop to complete one chain. When the required number of stitches have been worked into the ring, pull on the free end of the yarn to close the ring.

ch: chain

ch-sp(s): chain space(s)

dc: double crochet

dc5pop: (popcorn stitch) work 5dc in indicated st. Drop loop from hook. Insert hook from front to back through top of first dc of group. Grab dropped loop with hook and pull through st to close.

dtr: double treble crochet

inc: increase by making 2dc into the same stitch

rep: repeat

sc: single crochet

sc2tog: decrease 1 st by working 2sc together

sk: skip a stitch

sl st: slip stitch

st(s): stitch(es)

yo: yarn over

*: work following sequence of stitches; repeat sequence designated number of times more

( ): stitches between parentheses to be worked into the same stitch or space

Note

Chart shows Rounds 1–20 only and does not show beginning and end of rounds. See written instructions.

Join with a sl st after each round.

SHRUG

Make an adjustable ring.

Round 1
ch3 (counts as dc), 11dc in ring—12dc.

Round 2
ch3 (counts as first dc), dc in same st, *inc; rep from * around—24dc.

Round 3
ch 2 (counts as sc), *ch3, sk 1, sc, rep from * around—12 ch3-sps.

Round 4
sl st in ch3-sp, dc5pop in next ch-sp, using ch3 as first dc, ch3, *dc5pop, ch3; rep in from * around—12 dc5pop.

Round 5
ch7 (counts as sc, ch5), *sc in next dc5pop, ch5, rep from * around—12 ch5-sps.

Round 6
sl st in ch5-sp, ch 6 (counts as sc, ch4), sc in next ch5-sp, ch8, *sc in next ch5-sp, ch4, sc in ch5-sp, ch8, rep from * around—6 ch8-sps.

Round 7
sl st in ch4-sp, ch4 (counts as (sc, ch2), (8hdc, ch2, 8hdc) in ch8-sp, ch2, *sc in ch4-sp, ch2, (8hdc, ch2, 8hac) in ch8-sp, ch2; rep from * around.

Round 8
ch12 (counts as dtr, ch7), sk 8 hdc, sc in next ch2-sp, ch7, *dtr in next sc, ch7, sk 8 hdc, sc in next ch2-sp, ch7; rep from * around—12 ch7-sps.

Round 9
ch3 (counts as dc), 11dc in same ch7-sp, *(12dc) in next ch7-sp; rep from * around—144dc.

Rounds 10—11
ch3 (counts as first dc), dc in each dc around.

Round 12
ch5 (counts as sc, ch3), *ch3, sk1, sc; rep from * around—72 ch3-sps.

Rounds 13—14
sl st in ch-sp, ch5 (couts as sc, ch3), *ch3, sc in ch3-sp; rep from * around.

Round 15
ch3 (counts as first dc), (2dc), in same ch3-sp, *(3dc) in next ch3-sp; rep from * around—216dc.

Round 16
ch3 (counts as first dc), 10dc, inc, *11dc, inc; rep from * around—234dc.

Round 17
ch 3 (counts as first dc), dc in each dc around.

Round 18
ch5 (counts as sc, ch3), *ch3, sk 1, sc; rep from * around—117 ch3-sps.

Rounds 19—20
ch5 (counts as sc, ch3), sc in ch3-sp, ch3; rep from * around.

Round 21
ch 3 (counts as first dc), (2dc) in same ch3-sp, *(3dc) in next ch3-sp; rep from * around—351dc.

Round 22 (armholes)
ch3 (counts as dc), 75dc, ch30, sk30, 180dc, ch30, sk30, 35dc (this creates the armholes; they should line up with the points of the star in the mandala).

Round 23

ch3 (counts as dc), *75dc (30dc in ch30-sp), 180dc, (30dc in ch30-sp), 35dc—351dc.

Round 24

ch5 (counts as sc, ch3), sk1, sc2tog, ch3, *sk1, sc, ch3; rep from * around—175 ch3-sps.

Round 25—26

ch5 (counts as sc, ch3), *sc in ch3-sp, ch3; rep from * around.

Round 27

ch3 (counts as first dc), (2dc) in same ch3-sp, *(3dc) in next ch3-sp; rep from * around—525dc.

Round 28

ch3 (counts as first dc), dc in each dc around.

Rounds 29—32

Repeat round 28 four more times.

Round 33

ch5 (counts as sc, ch3), sk1, sc2tog, ch3, *sk1, sc, ch3; rep from * around—262 ch3-sps.

Round 34

ch5 (counts as sc, ch3), *sc in ch3-sp, ch3; rep from * around.

Round 35

ch5 (counts as sc, ch3), *sc in ch3-sp, ch3; rep from * around. Fasten off.

Finishing

Braid a few lengths of yarn to create a drawstring to tie the shrug.

FEATHERED DREAMS DREAM CATCHER

Ethereal and lovely, this dream catcher imbues its environment with peace. According to Ojibwe legend, dream catchers are magical spider webs that catch bad dreams and let good ones through.

Designed by Marinke Slump

Sample measures approximately:
8½in. x 8½in. (22cm x 22cm)
(not including feathers)

Materials

- Creative Linen by Rowan, 100g/3.5oz hanks, each approx. 219yd/200m (DK)
- 1 hank each in #625 Teal (A), 645 White (B), #626 Lilac (C), #629 Apple (D), #620 Cloud (E), #632 Leaf (F), #624 Foggy (G)
- Crochet hook size G-6 (4mm)
- A 9in./23cm diameter hoop
- 3 feathers

Stitches & Abbreviations

adjustable ring: Wrap the free end of the yarn twice around the index and third fingers of your left hand. With the hook and the yarn coming from the ball, draw a loop under the strands and into the ring. Yo and draw through the loop to complete one chain. When the required number of stitches have been worked into the ring, pull on the free end of the yarn to close the ring.

ch: chain

ch-sp(s): chain space(s)

dc: double crochet

dc5pop (popcorn stitch): work 5dc in indicated st. Drop loop from hook. Insert hook from front to back through top of first dc of group. Grab dropped loop with hook and pull through st to close.

inc: increase by making 2dc into the same stitch

rep: repeat

sc: single crochet

sk: skip a stitch

sl st: slip stitch

st(s): stitch(es)

rep: repeat

yo: yarn over

* : work following sequence of stitches; repeat sequence designated number of times more

( ): stitches between parentheses to be worked into the same stitch or space

Note

Join with a sl st after each round.

42

DREAM CATCHER

With A, make an adjustable ring.

Round 1
ch4 (counts as dc, ch1) *dc in ring, ch1; rep from *14 times more—16dc. Fasten off.

Round 2
Join B with sl st in 3rd ch of first ch4, ch5 (counts as dc, ch2), *dc, ch2; rep from * around. Fasten off.

Round 3
Join C with sl st in 3rd ch of first ch5, ch2 (counts as sc), (3sc) in next ch2-sp, *sc in next dc, (3sc) in next ch2-sp; rep from * around—64sc. Fasten off.

Round 4
Join D with sl st in middle sc in first ch2-sp, ch3, dc5pop in same sc as ch3 using ch 3 for first dc, ch3, sk3 sc, *dc5pop in next sc, ch3, sk3 sc; rep from * around—16 dc5pop. Fasten off.

Round 5
Join E with sl st in first ch3-sp, ch8 (counts as dc, ch 5), *dc in next ch3-sp, ch5; rep from * around. Fasten off—16 ch5-sps.

Round 6
Join F with sl st in first ch5sp, dc5pop using ch3 for first dc, ch4, *dc5pop in next ch5-sp, ch4; rep from * around—16 dc5pop. Fasten off.

Round 7
Join G with sl st to first ch4-sp, (ch3 (counts as dc), 2dc, ch2, 3dc in same ch4-sp), *(3dc, ch2, 3dc) in next ch4-sp; rep from * around. Fasten off.

Finishing
With B, work 10sc around the hoop, then sc through the ch2-sp from round 7. Rep until all ch2-sps are attached to the hoop.

Attach feathers and fringe along the bottom of the dream catcher, using the photo as a guide.

LEAVES AND BERRIES BAG

The perfect accessory for your summertime adventures in nature. The airy design is worked in lightweight linen, and the cross-body strap can be customized to the perfect length.

LEAVES AND BERRIES BAG

Designed by Marinke Slump

Sample measures 12¹/₂in. x 12¹/₂in. (32cm x 32cm)

Materials

- Creative Linen by Rowan, 100g/3.5oz hanks, each approx. 219yd/200m (DK)
- 1 hank each in #626 Lilac (A), #629 Apple (B), #632 Leaf (C), #624 Foggy (D), #635 Stormy (E)
- Crochet hook size C-2 or D-3 (3mm)
- Fabric to line the bag with (optional)
- A button (optional)

Stitches & Abbreviations

adjustable ring: Wrap the free end of the yarn twice around the index and third fingers of your left hand. With the hook and the yarn coming from the ball, draw a loop under the strands and into the ring. Yo and draw through the loop to complete one chain. When the required number of stitches have been worked into the ring, pull on the free end of the yarn to close the ring.

ch-sp(s): chain space(s)

ch: chain

dc: double crochet

dc5pop: popcorn stitch (work 5dc in indicated st. Drop loop from hook. Insert hook from front to back through top of first dc of group. Grab dropped loop with hook and pull through st to close.)

inc: increase by making 2dc into the same stitch

rep: repeat

sc: single crochet

tog: together

sk: skip a stitch

sl st: slip stitch

st(s): stitch(es)

yo: yarn over

*: work following sequence of stitches; repeat sequence designated number of times more

( ): stitches between parentheses to be worked into the same stitch or spaceace

Note

Chart does not show beginning and end of rounds. See written instructions.

Join with a sl st after each round.

BAG

With A, make an adjustable ring.

Round 1
ch3 (counts as dc), 11dc in ring—12dc.

Round 2
ch6 (counts as sc, ch4), sk 1, *sc, ch4, sk 1; rep from * around—6 ch4-sps.

Round 3
sl st in first ch4-sp, ch3 (counts as dc), (3dc) in same ch4-sp, ch3, *(4dc) in next ch4-sp, ch3; rep from * around—6 4dc-groups.

Round 4
ch3 (counts as dc), 3dc, (dc, ch2, sc, ch2, dc) in ch3-sp, *4dc, (dc, ch2, sc, ch2, dc) in ch3-sp; rep from * around—6 4dc-groups.

Round 5
ch3 (counts as dc), 3dc, ch2, sk 1, sc in ch2-sp, ch3, sk 1, sc in ch2-sp, ch2, sk 1, *4dc, ch2, sk 1, sc in ch2-sp, ch3, sk 1, sc in ch2-sp, ch2, sk 1; rep from * around—6 4dc-groups.

Round 6
ch3 (counts as dc), 3dc, dc in next ch-sp, ch3, sc in next ch-sp, ch3, dc in next ch-sp, *4dc, dc in next ch-sp, ch3, sc in next ch-sp, ch3, dc in next ch-sp; rep from * around—12 ch3-sps.

Round 7
ch3 (counts as dc), 4dc, 3dc in next ch-sp, ch1, 3dc in next ch-sp, *6dc, 3dc in next ch-sp, ch1, 3dc in next ch-sp; rep from * 4 times more, dc in last dc—6 ch1-sps.

Round 8
ch 3 (counts as dc), 7dc, 2dc in ch-sp, *12dc, 2dc in ch sp; rep from * 4 times more, 4dc—84 dc.

Round 9
sl st in 2sts, ch5 (counts as sc, ch3), sk2, *sc, ch3, sk2; rep from * around—28 ch3-sps. Fasten off.

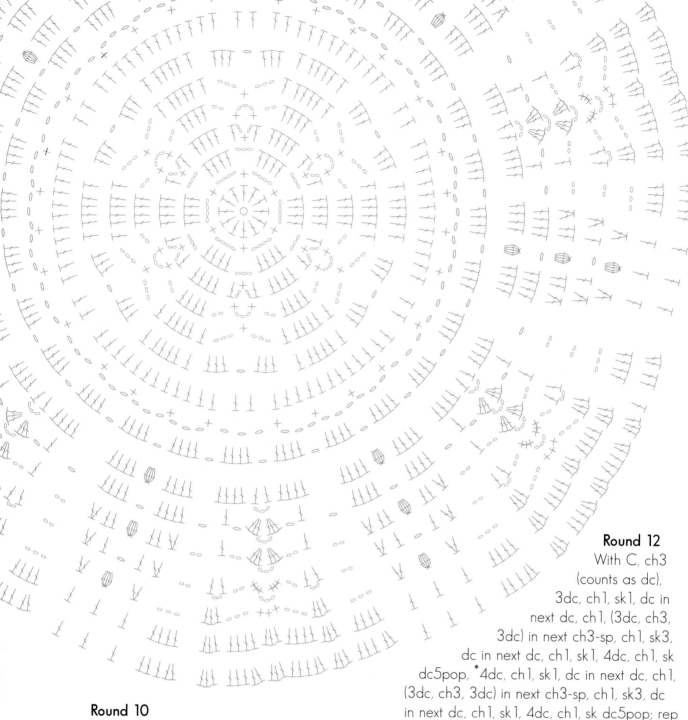

Round 10

Join B in first ch-sp, ch 3 (counts as dc), (3dc) in same ch-sp, ch1, *(4dc) in next ch sp, ch1; rep from * around—28 4dc-groups.

Round 11

ch3 (counts as dc), 3dc, sk ch-sp, 4dc, (dc, ch3, dc) in ch-sp, 4dc, sk ch-sp, 4dc, dc5pop in ch-sp, *4dc, sk ch-sp, 4dc, (dc, ch3, dc) in ch-sp, 4dc, sk ch-sp, 4dc, dc5pop in ch-sp; rep from * around, changing to C in last dc5pop—7 dc5pop. Cut B.

Round 12

With C, ch3 (counts as dc), 3dc, ch1, sk1, dc in next dc, ch1, (3dc, ch3, 3dc) in next ch3-sp, ch1, sk3, dc in next dc, ch1, sk1, 4dc, ch1, sk dc5pop, *4dc, ch1, sk1, dc in next dc, ch1, (3dc, ch3, 3dc) in next ch3-sp, ch1, sk3, dc in next dc, ch1, sk1, 4dc, ch1, sk dc5pop; rep from * around.

Round 13

ch3 (counts as first dc), dc, dc2tog, ch2, sk ch-sp, dc, ch2, sk ch-sp, (3dc, ch3, 3dc) in next ch-sp, ch2, sk ch-sp, dc, ch2, sk ch-sp, dc2tog, 2dc, dc5pop in ch-sp, *2dc, dc2tog, ch2, sk ch-sp, dc, ch 2, sk ch-sp, (3dc, ch3, 3dc) in next ch-sp, ch2, sk ch-sp, dc, ch2, sk ch-sp, dc2tog, 2dc, dc5pop in ch-sp; rep from * around, changing to D in last dc5pop. Cut C.

Round 14

With D, ch3 (counts as dc), dc2tog, ch2, sk ch-sp, (dc, ch2, dc) in next dc, ch2, sk ch-sp, (3sc, ch3, 3sc) in next ch-sp, ch2, sk ch-sp, (dc, ch2, dc) in next dc, ch2, sk ch-sp, dc2tog, dc, ch1, sk dc5-pop, *dc in next dc, dc2tog, ch2, sk ch-sp, (dc, ch2, dc) in next dc, ch2, sk ch-sp, (3sc, ch3, 3sc) in next ch-sp, ch2, sk ch-sp, (dc, ch2, dc) in next dc, ch2, sk ch-sp, dc2tog, dc, ch1, sk dc5pop; rep from * around.

Round 15

dc2tog (using ch3 for first dc), ch3, sk ch-sp, (3dc) in next ch-sp, ch3, sk ch-sp, (3sc) in next ch-sp, ch3, sk ch-sp, (3dc) in next ch-sp, ch3, sk ch-sp, dc2tog, dc5pop in ch-sp, *dc2tog, ch3, sk ch-sp, (3dc) in next ch-sp, ch3, sk ch-sp, (3sc) in next ch-sp, ch3, sk ch-sp, (3dc) in next ch-sp, ch3, sk ch-sp, dc2tog, dc5pop in ch-sp; rep from * around, changing to E in last dc5pop. Cut D.

Round 16

With E, ch3 (counts as dc), (4dc) in ch-sp, *3dc, (4dc) in ch-sp; rep from * around, end 2dc—196dc.

Round 17

ch3 (counts as dc), 3dc, inc, *6dc, inc; rep from * around, end 2dc—224dc. Fasten off.

THE BAG HANDLE

The handle is worked in rows. Start from the same side each time; do not turn your work.

With E, ch the desired length of the handle (it should wrap around the bag and your shoulder). You should have an even number of stitches.

Row 1

Sc in 2nd ch from hook and in each ch across. Fasten off.

Row 2

Join D in first sc, ch1, sc in same st, ch1, sk1, *sc, ch1, sk1; rep from * across. Fasten off.

Row 3

Join B in first sc, ch1, sc in same st, *sc in ch-sp, ch1; rep from * across, sc in last sc. Fasten off.

Row 4

With C, Repeat row 3.

Rows 5–8

Rep rows 3 and 4 two more times.

Row 9

With B, rep row 3.

Row 10

With D, rep row 3.

Row 11

Join E in first sc, ch2 (counts as hdc), hdc in each st across. Fasten off. Sew in the ends.

Attach the handle to the bag with a single crochet stitch through the back loops only. Line the bag and attach a button loop and button (optional).

TWILIGHT HOOK CASE

An interesting take on mandalas, this hook case combines a spiral mandala motif with pieces that are crocheted straight across. Lace weight yarn, worked tightly, keeps your crochet hooks secure.

TWILIGHT HOOK CASE

Designed by Anita Mundt

Sample measures as follows: the finished rectangle is 6¹/₂in. x 7in. (16cm x 18cm) and the diameter of the spiral mandalas is 2¹/₂in. (6cm)

Materials

- Rialto Lace by Debbie Bliss, 50g/1.75oz balls, each approx. 426yd/390m (lace) Small amounts each in #20 Indigo (A), #19 Royal (B), and #7 Fuschia (C)
- Crochet hook size C-2 (2.75mm)
- 2cm x 2cm buttons
- Sewing thread
- Sewing needle

Stitches & Abbreviations

ch: chain

ch7pc: ch7, sl st in base of first ch to form picot

dc: double crochet

hdc: half double crochet

sl st: slip stitch

sc: single crochet

st(s): stitch(es)

*: work following sequence of stitches; repeat sequence designated number of times more

( ): stitches between parentheses to be worked into the same stitch or space

Note

Make 2 spiral mandalas to act as the top and bottom of your case, and one rectangle as the body of the case.

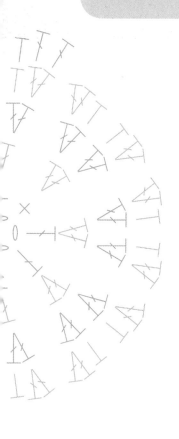

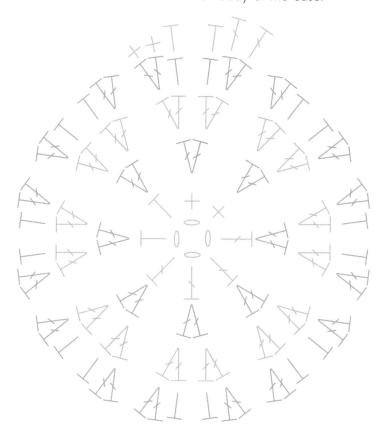

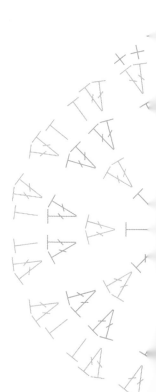

HOOK CASE

SPIRAL MANDALA (make two)

With one strand each of A and B held together, ch4, sl st to first ch to form a ring.

Round 1
Working in ring, ch2 (counts as first sc), sc, 2hdc, 4dc; do not join—8sts.

Round 2
Working around in a spiral, (2dc) in top of ch2 of previous round, *(2dc) in next stitch; rep from * 6 times more—16sts.

Round 3
(not shown on chart) (2dc) in first st of previous round, *(2dc) in next stitch; rep from * repeat 14 times more—32sts.

Round 4
(2dc) in first st of previous round, 2hdc, (2dc) in next st, *(2dc) in next stitch, 2hdc, (2dc) in next st; rep from * 6 times more—48sts.

Round 5
dc in first st of previous round, dc, 2hdc, 2sc, sl st. Fasten off.

SPIRAL MANDALA DETAIL

Using 1 strand of color C, join with a loop to the center of the mandala. Using surface chain stitches follow the spiral of the mandala. Make a slip stitch

when you get to the outer edge and fasten off the yarn.

RECTANGLE

With 1 strand each of A, B, and C held together, ch34.

Rows 1–28
ch2, counts as hdc, hdc in each st across—34sts.

Row 29 (to make the button loops) ch2, 12hdc, ch7pc, 10hdc, ch7pc, 12hdc. Fasten off.

Finishing
Sew the mandalas to the top and bottom edge of the rectangle leaving the foundation chain and the button loop row open, with the loops overlapping the foundation chain. Sew buttons to align with the loops.

FRUIT PICKER'S VEST

Vintage design elements, like patchwork construction and long fringe, combine with a modern color palette to create a cool and beautiful vest. Crocheted in Debbie Bliss Blue Faced Leicester, it wears beautifully and is comfortable against the skin.

FRUIT PICKER'S VEST

Designed by Marinke Slump

Gauge: 22 rows x 30 sts = 4in. (10cm)
Sample Measures 17½in. (44cm) across back panel and 18in. (46cm) long without fringe.

Materials

- Blue Faced Leicester Aran by Debbie Bliss, 50g/1.75oz balls, each approx. 82yd/75m (aran)
- 4 balls in #8 Rose (A),
- 2 balls each in #15 Sage (B), and #16 Willow (C)
- 1 ball in #1 Ecru (D)
- Crochet hook size H-8 (5mm)

Stitches & Abbreviations

adjustable ring: Wrap the free end of the yarn twice around the index and third fingers of your left hand. With the hook and the yarn coming from the ball, draw a loop under the strands and into the ring. Yo and draw through the loop to complete one chain. When the required number of stitches have been worked into the ring, pull on the free end of the yarn to close the ring.

ch: chain

ch-sp(s): chain space(s)

dc: double crochet

hdc: half double crochet

rep: repeat

sc: single crochet

sl st: slip stitch

st(s): stitch(es)

pf (puff stitch): (yo, insert hook into stitch and pull up a loop) 3 times, yo and pull through all loops on hook

pf2tog: (puff stitch decrease) (yo, insert hook into stitch and pull up a loop) 3 times, (yo, insert hook into next stitch, and pull up a loop) 3 times, yo and pull through all loops on hook

yo: yarn over

*: work following sequence of stitches; repeat sequence designated number of times more

( ): stitches between parentheses to be worked into the same stitch or space

Note

Chart does not show beginning and end of rounds. See written instructions.

Round 3

With B, ch2 (does not count as stitch), *3pf, ch2; rep from * around. Join with sl st to first pf—24pf.

Round 4

ch 2 (does not count as a st), *1pf, pf2tog, ch5, sk ch2-sp; rep from * around. Join with sl st to first pf—16pf.

Round 5

ch 2 (does not count as a st), *pf2tog, ch4, dc in ch-sp, ch4; rep from * around. Join with a sl st to top of first pf2tog—8pf. Fasten off.

Round 6

Join C in any pf2tog, then ch6 (counts as first sc, ch 4), hdc in dc, ch4, (2dc, ch2, 2dc) in next pf2tog, ch4, hdc in dc, ch4, *sc in next pf2tog, ch4, hdc in dc, ch4, (2dc, ch2, 2dc) in next pf2tog, ch4, hdc in dc, ch4; rep from * around. Join with sl st to first sc. Fasten off.

VEST

MOTIF (make fifteen)

With A, make an adjustable ring.

Round 1

ch4 (counts as dc and ch1), *dc in ring, ch1; rep from * 6 times. Join with sl st to 3rd ch of first ch4—8dc and ch1-sps.

Round 2

sl st in ch-sp, ch3 (counts as first dc), (2dc) in same ch1-sp, *(3dc) in each ch1-sp around, changing to B in last dc. Join with sl st to top of first ch3—24dc. Cut A.

Finishing

Using nine motifs for the back and three for each front, join motifs with D and sc through back loops only from the right side. Leave the sides open at the top square for armholes (see photo). Finish the vest by working single crochet around the neck and armholes with B, working sc in each stitch, 5sc in each ch4-sp, and 2sc into each ch2-sp at corners. Crochet an edge along the bottom the same way, but using dc stitches instead. Use D to tie fringe along the bottom of the vest.

RIDGED WAVES TABLE COVER

A bright fix to spruce up a plain table or stool, the clever use of front-post crochet stitches give the Ridged Waves Table Cover a modern, angular look.

RIDGED WAVES TABLE COVER

Designed by Marinke Slump

Sample measures 16in. x 16in. (40cm x 40cm)

Materials

- Softknit Cotton by Rowan, 50g/1.75oz balls, each approx. 115yd/105m (worsted)
- 1 ball each in #525 Lupin (A), #585 Indigo Blue (B), #579 Dark Lime (C), and #571 Sand (D)
- Crochet hook size G-6 (4mm)

Stitches & Abbreviations

adjustable ring: Wrap the free end of the yarn twice around the index and third fingers of your left hand. With the hook and the yarn coming from the ball, draw a loop under the strands and into the ring. Yo and draw through the loop to complete a chain. When the required number of stitches have been worked into the ring, pull on the free end of the yarn to close the ring.

ch: chain

ch-sp(s): chain space(s)

dc: double crochet

fpdc: front post double crochet. Yo and insert hook aound post of next dc from front to back, yo and draw up a loop, (yo and draw through 2 loops) twice.

rep: repeat

sk: skip a stitch

sl st: slip stitch

st(s): stitch(es)

yo: yarn over

*: work following sequence of stitches; repeat sequence designated number of times

( ): stitches between parentheses to be worked into the same stitch or space

Note

Join with a sl st after each round.

TABLE COVER

With A, make an adjustable ring.

Round 1
ch4 (counts as dc, ch 1) *dc, ch1; rep from
* 10 times more in ring—12dc. Fasten off.

Round 2
Join B in any ch1-sp, ch3 (counts as dc), fpdc
around dc, dc in ch1-sp, ch5 loosely, *dc in
next ch1-sp, fpdc around dc, dc in next ch1-
sp, ch5 loosely; rep from * around—18dc.
Fasten off.

Round 3
Join A in joining sl st, ch3 (counts as dc) dc in
same dc, fpdc around fpdc, (2dc) in next dc,
ch5 loosely, *(2dc) in next dc, fpdc around
fpdc, (2dc) in next dc, ch5 loosely; rep from *
around—30dc.

Round 4
ch3 (counts as dc), dc in same dc, dc, fpdc
around fpdc, dc, (2dc) in next dc, ch5 loosely,
*(2dc) in next dc, dc, fpdc around fpdc, dc,
(2dc) in next dc, ch5 loosely; rep from * around.
Fasten off—42dc.

Round 5
Join C in joining sl st, ch3 (counts as dc), dc in
same dc, 2dc, fpdc around fpdc, 2dc, (2dc)
in next dc, ch5 loosely, *(2dc) in next dc, 2dc,
fpdc around fpdc, 2dc, (2dc) in next dc, ch5
loosely; rep from * around—54dc. Fasten off.

Round 6
Join A in joining sl st, ch3 (counts
as dc), dc in same dc, 3dc, fpdc
around fpdc, 3dc, (2dc) in dc,
ch5 loosely, *(2dc) in next dc, 3dc,
fpdc around fpdc, 3dc, (2dc) in
dc, ch5 loosely; rep from * around.
Fasten off—66dc.

Round 7

Join C in joining sl st, ch3 (counts as dc), dc in same dc, 4dc, fpdc around fpdc, 4dc, (2dc) in next dc, ch5 loosely, *(2dc) in next dc, 4dc, fpdc around fpdc, 4dc, (2dc) in next dc, ch5 loosely; rep from * around—78dc.

Round 8

ch3 (counts as dc), dc in same dc, 5dc, fpdc around fpdc, 5dc, (2dc) in next dc, ch5 loosely, *(2dc) in next dc, 5dc, fpdc around fpdc, 5dc, (2dc) in next dc, ch5 loosely; rep from * around. Fasten off—90dc.

Round 9

Join D in joining sl st, ch3 (counts as dc), dc in same dc, 6dc, fpdc around fpdc, 6dc, (2dc) in next dc, ch5 loosely,*(2dc) in next dc, 6dc, fpdc around fpdc, 6dc, (2dc) in next dc, ch5 loosely; rep from * around. Fasten off—102dc.

Round 10

Join C in joining sl st, ch3 (counts as dc), dc in same dc, 7dc, fpdc around fpdc, 7dc, (2dc) in next dc, ch5 loosely, *(2dc) in next dc, 7dc, fpdc around fpdc, 7dc, (2dc) in next dc, ch5 loosely; rep from * around. Fasten off—114dc.

Round 11

Join D in joining sl st, ch3 (counts as dc), dc in same dc, 8dc, fpdc around fpdc, 8dc, (2dc) in next dc, ch5 loosely, *(2dc) in next dc, 8dc, fpdc around fpdc, 8dc, (2dc) in next dc, ch5 loosely; rep from * around—126dc.

Round 12

ch3 (counts as dc), dc in same dc, 9dc, fpdc around fpdc, 9dc, (2dc) in next dc, ch5 loosely, *(2dc) in next dc, 9dc, fpdc around fpdc, 9dc, (2dc) in next dc, ch5 loosely; rep from * around. Fasten off—138dc.

Round 13

Join B in joining sl st, ch3 (counts as dc), dc in same dc, 10dc, fpdc around fpdc, 10dc, (2dc) in dc, ch5 loosely, *(2dc) in dc, 10dc, fpdc around fpdc, 10dc, (2dc) in dc, ch5 loosely; rep from * around— 150dc. Fasten off.

Round 14

Join D in joining sl st, ch3 (counts as dc), dc in same dc, 11dc, fpdc around fpdc, 11dc, (2dc) in next dc, ch5 loosely, *(2dc) in next dc, 11dc, fpdc around fpdc, 11dc, (2dc) in next dc, ch5 loosely; rep from * around—162dc. Fasten off.

Round 15

Join B in joining sl st, ch3 (counts as dc), dc in same dc, 12dc, fpdc around fpdc, 12dc, (2dc) in next dc, ch5 loosely, *(2dc) in next dc, 12dc, fpdc around fpdc, 12dc, (2dc) in next dc, ch5 loosely; rep from * around—174dc.

Round 16

ch3 (counts as dc), dc in same dc, 13dc, fpdc around fpdc, 13dc, (2dc) in dc, ch5 loosely, *(2dc) in next dc, 13dc, fpdc around fpdc, 13dc, (2dc) in dc, ch5 loosely; rep from * around. Fasten off—186dc. Beginning at the center, weave the ch5-loops: pull the second loop through the first loop, pull the third loop through the second loop, continue weaving loops outwards in this way.

Round 17

Join A in joining sl st, dc in same dc, 14dc, fpdc around fpdc, 14dc, (2dc) in next dc, dc in ch5-loop, *(2dc) in next dc, 14dc, fpdc around fpdc, 14dc, (2dc) in next dc, dc in ch5-loop; rep from * around. Fasten off.

Round 18

Join B in joining sl st, dc in same dc, 15dc, dc in fpdc, 15dc, (2dc) in next dc, (2dc) in next dc, *(2dc) in next dc, 15dc, dc in fpdc, 15dc, (2dc) in next dc, (2dc) in next dc; rep from * around. Fasten off. Block into shape.

DOILY RAG RUG

Breathe new life into your old linens and garments. The Doily Rag Rug can be made with materials you already have in your home, making it a budget-friendly, nostalgic, and stylish project.

DOILY RAG RUG

Designed by Marinke Slump

Sample measures approximately
55in. x 55in. (140cm x 140cm)

Materials

- Crochet hook size Q-19 (15mm)
- 3 vintage sheets ripped into strips
  1in./2.5cm wide

Stitches & Abbreviations

adjustable ring: Wrap the free end of the yarn
twice around the index and third fingers of your
left hand. With the hook and the yarn coming
from the ball, draw a loop under the strands
and into the ring. Yo and draw through the

loop to complete one chain. When the required
number of stitches have been worked into the
ring, pull on the free end of the yarn to close
the ring.

ch: chain

ch-sp(s): chain space(s)

dc: double crochet

inc: increase by making 2dc into the same stitch

rep: repeat

sl st: slip stitch

st(s): stitch(es)

yo: yarn over

*: work following sequence of stitches; repeat
sequence designated number of times more

( ): stitches between parentheses to be worked
into the same stitch or space

RUG

Make an adjustable ring.

Round 1
ch3 (counts as first dc), 11dc in ring. Join with sl st to top of first ch3—12dc.

Round 2
ch3 (counts as first dc), dc in same st, (2dc) in each st around. Join with sl st to top of first ch3—24dc.

Round 3
ch3 (counts as first dc), inc, *dc, inc; rep from * around. Join with sl st to top of first ch3—36dc.

Round 4
ch3 (counts as first dc), dc, inc, *2dc, inc; rep from * around. Join with sl st to top of first ch3—48dc.

Round 5
ch3 (counts as first dc), 2dc, inc, *3dc, inc; rep from * around. Join with sl st to top of first ch3—60dc.

Round 6
ch3 (counts as first dc), 3dc, inc, *4dc, inc; rep from * around. Join with sl st to top of first ch3—72dc.

Round 7
ch3 (counts as first dc), 4dc, inc, *5dc, inc; rep from * around. Join with sl st to top of first ch3—84dc.

Round 8
ch3 (counts as first dc), 5dc, inc, *6dc, inc; rep from * around. Join with sl st to top of first ch3—96dc.

Round 9
ch3 (counts as first dc), 6dc, inc, *7dc, inc; rep from * around. Join with sl st to top of first ch3—108dc.

Round 10
ch3 (counts as first dc), 7dc, inc, *8dc, inc; rep from * around. Join with sl st to top of first ch3—120dc.

Round 11

ch3 (counts as first dc), 8dc, inc, *9dc, inc;
rep from * around. Join with sl st to top of first
ch3—132dc.

Round 12

ch3 (counts as first dc), 9dc, inc, *10dc, inc;
rep from * around. Join with sl st to top of first
ch3—144dc.

Round 13

ch3 (counts as first dc), 10dc, inc, *11dc, inc;
rep from * around. Join with sl st to top of first
ch3—156dc. Fasten off.

You can use the remainder of the fabric strips
to tie fringe to the rug.

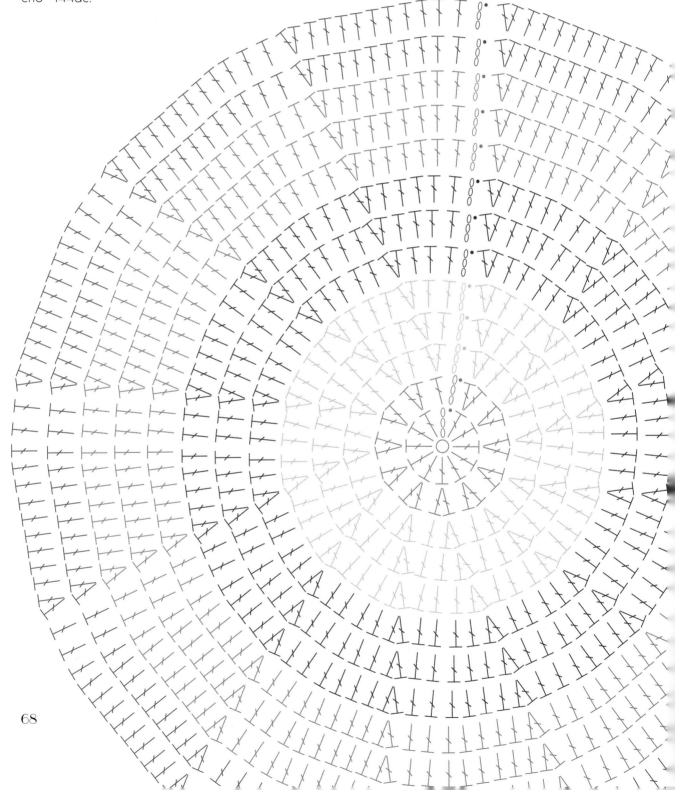

VIOLET NEEDLE CASE

The base of this needle case is made of felt, a sturdy anchor that allows you to create a lacy, intricate, crocheted overlay while keeping your needles secure. You can choose a felt color similar to your yarn, or choose something bright for contrast.

VIOLET NEEDLE CASE

Designed by Anita Mundt

Sample measures 8in. (20cm)

Materials

- Rialto Lace by Debbie Bliss, 50g/1.75oz balls, each approx. 426yd/390m (lace) Small amounts each in #20 Indigo (A) and #19 Royal (B)
- Crochet hook size C-2 (2.75mm)
- One 1in. (25mm) button
- Sewing thread
- Sewing needle
- One piece of felt 6in. x 6³⁄₄in./15cm x 17cm

Stitches & Abbreviations

ch: chain
ch-sp(s): chain space(s)
dc: double crochet
hdc: half double crochet
sl st: slip stitch
sc: single crochet
tr: treble crochet
rep: repeat
st(s): stitch(es)
***:** work following sequence of stitches; repeat sequence designated number of times more
( ): stitches between parentheses to be worked into the same stitch or space

Note: Chart does not show the beginning and ending of the rounds. See written instructions.

NEEDLE CASE

With A, ch6, sl st to form a ring.

Round 1
ch3 (counts as first dc), 11dc in ring, sl st to top of first ch3 to join—12dc.

Round 2
ch5 (counts as first sc, ch3), *sc in next dc, ch3; rep from * 10 times more, sl st to 2nd ch of ch5 to join—12 ch3-sps.

Round 3
sl st in first ch-sp, ch3 (counts as first dc), 2dc in same ch-sp, ch1, *3dc in next ch-sp, ch1; rep from * 10 times more, sl st to top of first ch3 to join—36dc. Fasten off.

Round 4
Join B in first ch-sp, ch6 (counts as first sc, ch4), *sc in next ch-sp, ch4* repeat 10 times more, sl st to top of first ch2 to join—12sc.

Round 5
ch1 (counts as first sl st), (2sc, 2dc, 2tr) in next ch-sp, ch1, (2tr, 2dc, 2sc) in next ch-sp, *sl st in next sc, (2sc, 2dc, 2tr) in next ch-sp, ch1 (2tr, 2dc, 2sc) in next ch-sp; rep from * 4 times more, sl st to top of first ch to join—6sl sts. Fasten off.

Round 6
Join A in first sl st of previous round, ch14 (counts as first sc, ch12), *sc in next sl st, ch12; rep from * 4 times more, sl st to top of first ch2 to join—6 ch12-sps.

Round 7
ch2 (counts as first sc), (12dc) in next ch-sp, *sc in next sc, (12dc) in next ch-sp; rep from * 4 times more, sl st to top of first ch2 to join—72sc.

Round 8
ch2 (counts as first sc), 2sc, 2dc, 2tr, ch2, skip 2dc, 2tr, 2dc, 2sc, *sc in next sc, 2sc, 2dc, 2tr, ch2, skip 2dc, 2tr, 2dc, 2sc; rep from * 4 times more, sl st to top of first ch2 to join—6 ch-2 sps. Fasten off.

Round 9
Join B in first ch2-sp, ch22 (counts as first sc, ch20) *sc in next ch2-sp, ch20; rep from * 4 times more, sl st to top of first ch2 to join—6 ch20-sps.

Round 10
ch2 (counts as first sc), 20dc in ch-sp, *sc in next sc, 20dc in next ch-sp; rep from * 4 times more, sl st to top of first ch2 to join—120dc.

Round 11

ch2 (counts as first sc), 2sc, 2hdc, 3dc, 3tr, ch20 for button loop, skip 2 dc, 3tr, 3dc, 2hdc, 2sc, *sc in next sc, 2sc, 2hdc, 3dc, 3tr, ch2 skip 2 dc, 3tr, 3dc, 2hdc, 2sc; rep from *4 times more, sl st to top of first ch2 to join. Fasten off.

Finishing

Fold the felt piece in half, round the corners and sew the center of the mandala along the fold line. Sew the points of your mandala to the felt. Wrap the ch20 loop around the open edge of the felt and secure with a button.

FLOWER IN THE SUN PINCUSHION

A pretty, palm-sized project, the Flower in the Sun Pincushion comes together quickly. As beautiful as it is practical, it's a welcome addition to any sewing table.

FLOWER IN THE SUN PINCUSHION

Designed by Anita Mundt

Sample measures 4in. (10cm) in diameter

Materials

- Pearl Cotton Balls #8 by DMC USA, 10g/.35oz balls, each approx. 87yd/80m (thread)
- Small amounts in #891 Dark Carnation (A), #600 Very Dark Cranberry (B), #943 Medium Aquamarine (C), #912 Light Emerald Green (D), #725 Topaz (E)
- Crochet hook size 12 steel(1mm)
- 2 pieces of felt approx. 4³/₄in./12cm diameter
- A handful of polyester stuffing
- Sewing thread and needle
- The bottom or top of a decorative tin approximately 4in./10cm diameter

Stitches & Abbreviations

adjustable ring: Wrap the free end of the yarn twice around the index and third fingers of your left hand. With the hook and the yarn coming from the ball, draw a loop under the strands and into the ring. Yo and draw through the loop to complete one chain. When the required number of stitches have been worked into the ring, pull on the free end of the yarn to close the ring.

ch: chain

ch-sp(s): chain space(s)

dc: double crochet

dc-cl: double crochet cluster (work 6dc to the last yo into the same stitch or space and join together by drawing final yo through all loops on hook)

hdc: half double crochet

rep: repeat

sc: single crochet

sl st: slip stitch

st(s): stitch(es)

tr: treble crochet

yo: yarn over

*: work following sequence of stitches; repeat sequence designated number of times more

( ): stitches between these parentheses to be worked into the same stitch or space

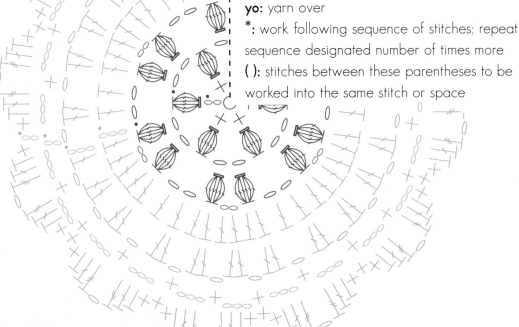

PINCUSHION

With A, make an adjustable ring.

Round 1
ch2 (counts as first sc), 5sc in ring, sl st to top of first ch2 to join—6sc.

Round 2
dc-cl (using ch3 as first dc), ch2, *dc-cl in next sc, ch2; rep from *4 times more, sl st to top of first dc-cl to join—6dc-cl. Fasten off.

Round 3
Join B in first ch-sp, dc-cl (using ch3 as first dc), ch2, dc-cl in same ch-sp, ch2, *(dc-cl, ch2, dc-cl) in next ch-sp, ch2; rep from *4 times more, sl st to top of first dc-cl to join—12dc-cl. Fasten off.

Round 4
Join C in first dc-cl, ch3 (counts as first dc), dc in same dc-cl, (2dc) in next ch-sp, *(2dc) in next dc-cl, (2dc) in next ch-sp; rep from *10 times more, changing to D in last dc, sl st to top of first ch3 to join—48dc. Cut B.

Round 6
Join E in first ch-sp, ch5 (counts as first sc, ch3), *sc in next ch-sp, ch3; rep from * repeat 22 times more, sl st to top of first ch2 to join—24sc.

Round 7
ch2 (counts as first sc), (sc, hdc, dc, tr) in next ch-sp, ch1, (tr, dc, hdc, sc) in next ch-sp, *sc in next sc, (sc, hdc, dc, tr) in next ch-sp, ch1, (tr, dc, hdc, sc) in next ch-sp; rep from * 10 times more, ending with sl st to top of first ch2 to join. Fasten off.

Finishing
Cut 2 circles from felt 1/2in./1cm bigger than your mandala. Sew the circles together leaving a 1/2in./1cm seam allowance and a 2in./5cm gap for turning the seamed circle inside out. Turn the seamed circle inside out so the stitching is on the inside. Stuff with polyester stuffing. Sew the gap closed. Stitch the mandala to one side of the stuffed felt circle. Place the pincushion in your decorative tin.

Round 5
With D, ch3 (counts as first dc), dc in same dc, ch1, skip next dc, *(2dc) in next dc, ch1, skip next dc; rep from * 22 times more, sl st to top of first ch3 to join—24 ch1-sps. Fasten off.

SEASHELL COASTERS

Simple and sweet, the saturated colors used for these coasters are balanced by delicate white picots. Worked in a cotton blend, they absorb liquid easily and hold up through hand washing.

Materials

- Softknit Cotton by Rowan, 50g/1.75oz balls, each approx. 115yd/105m (worsted)
- 1 hank each in #570 cream (A) and #575 Lupin (B) or #571 Sand (B) or #581 Seaweed (B) or #580 Marina (B)
- Crochet hook size G-6 (4mm)

SEASHELL COASTERS

Designed by Marinke Slump

Samples measure 4³/₄in. x 6¹/₂in. (12cm x 16cm)

Stitches & Abbreviations

adjustable ring: Wrap the free end of the yarn twice around the index and third fingers of your left hand. With the hook and the yarn coming from the ball, draw a loop under the strands and into the ring. Yo and draw through the loop to complete one chain. When the required number of stitches have been worked into the ring, pull on the free end of the yarn to close the ring.

ch: chain

ch-sp(s): chain space(s)

dc: double crochet

dtr: double treble crochet

pf (puff stitch): [yo, insert into stitch and pull up a loop] 3 times, yo and pull through all loops on hook

rep: repeat

sc: single crochet

sk: skip a stitch

sl st: slip stitch

st: stitch

tr: treble crochet

yo: yarn over

*: work following sequence of stitches; repeat sequence designated number of times more

( ): stitches between parentheses to be worked into the same stitch or space

Note: Chart does not show beginning and end of rounds. See written instructions.

Join with a sl st after each round.

COASTER

With B, make an adjustable ring.

Round 1
ch 3 (counts as dc), 11dc in ring, changing to A in lastdc—12 dc. Cut B.

Round 2
With A, ch3, (counts as sc, ch1), *sc in next dc, ch1; rep from * around—12sc. Fasten off.

Round 3
Join B in first ch1-sp, ch1 (does not count as a st), *pf in ch1-sp, ch1; rep from * around—12pf. Fasten off.

Round 4
Join A in first ch1-sp, ch4 (counts as sc, ch2), *sc in next ch1-sp, ch2; rep from * around—12 ch2-sps. Fasten off.

Round 5
Join B in first ch2-sp, ch1 (counts as first sc) (3sc) in same ch-2sp, (4sc) in next 4 ch-sps, (4hdc) in next 2 ch-sps, (4dc, tr) in next ch-sp, (tr, 4dc) in next ch-sp, (4hdc) in next 2 ch-sps, (4sc) in next ch-sp—12 goups of sts. Fasten off.

Round 6
Join A between first and last group of sts, ch5 (counts as sc, ch3), *sc between next 2 groups of sts, ch3; rep from * around—12 ch3-sps. Fasten off.

Round 7
Join B in first ch-sp, ch2 (counts as hdc) (4hdc) in same ch-sp, (5hdc) in next 4 ch-sps, (5dc) in next 2 ch-sps, (4tr, 3dtr) in next ch-sp, ch1, (3dtr, 4tr) in next ch-sp, (5dc) in next 2ch-sps, (5hdc) in next ch-sp, changing to A in last hdc. Cut B.

Round 8
With A, ch2 (counts as sc), 3sc, (sc, ch3, sc) in next st, *4sc, (sc, ch3, sc) in next st; rep from * 5 times more, 3sc, (sc, ch3, sc) in next st, 3sc, (sc, ch3, sc) in ch-sp, 3sc, (sc, ch3, sc) in next st, 7sc, (sc, ch3, sc) in next st, 4sc, (sc, ch3, sc) in next st, 4sc, (sc, ch3, sc) in next st. Fasten off. Block into shape.

SINGING DAISIES GARLAND

A clever crocheted take on bunting, the Singing Daisies Garland is a unique decorative piece. The bold daisy pattern draws the eye, while gold accent beads catch the light. Customize the garland by playing with the garland length and fasteners.

SINGING DAISIES GARLAND

Designed by Anita Mundt

Sample mandala measures 11 in. (28cm) in diameter

Materials

- Baby Cashmerino by Debbie Bliss, 50g/1.75oz balls, each approx. 137yd/125m (sport)
- 20g/small amounts each in #02 Apple, #03 Light Lime, #10 Lilac, #26 Seafoam, #79 Purple, #80 Jade, #102 Beige, #203 Teal
- One ribbon 1.5m/1.5yd long
- 80 small bells
- 16 wooden clothespins
- Crochet hook size D-3 (3.25 mm)

Stitches & Abbreviations

ch: chain

ch-sp(s): chain space(s)

ch5pc (picot using 5 chain stitches): ch5, sl st in first ch to form picot

d-dc-dec: decrease 2 stitches by joining 3 double crochets together by working each dc to the last yo, then joining by drawing last yo through all loops on hook

dc-dec: decrease a stitch by joining 2 double crochets together by working each dc to the last yo, then joining by drawing last yo through all loops on hook

dc: double crochet

hdc: half double crochet

rep: repeat

sc: single crochet

sk: skip

sl st: slip stitch

st(s): stitch(es)

tr: treble crochet

*: work following sequence of stitches; repeat sequence designated number of times more

( ): stitches between these parentheses to be worked into the same stitch or space

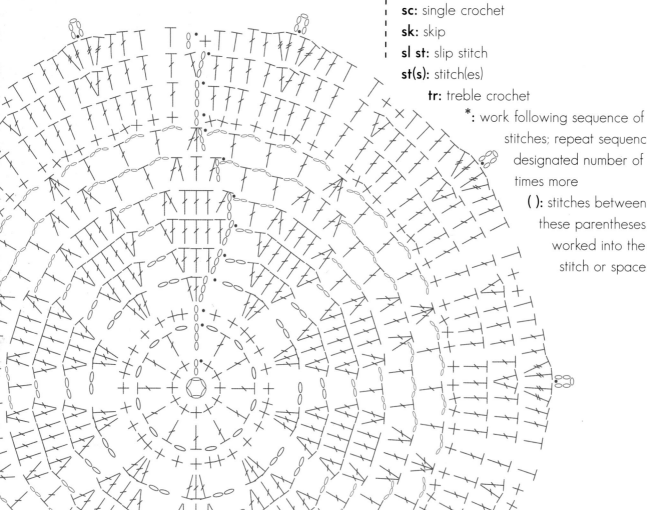

GARLAND

MANDALA (make eight, one in each color)

Thread 10 small bells onto yarn before you begin.

ch6, join with sl st to form a ring.

Round 1
ch2 (counts as first sc), 11 sc in ring, sl st to top of first ch2 to join—12sc.

Round 2
ch4 (counts as first dc, ch1), *dc, ch1; rep from * repeat 10 times more, sl st to top of first ch3 to join—12dc.

Round 3
ch2 (counts as first sc), 2sc in next ch-sp, *sc in next dc, sc in ch-sp, sc in next dc, 2sc in ch-sp; rep from * 4 times more, sc in next dc, sc in ch-sp, sl st to top of first ch2 to join—30sc.

Round 4
ch3 (counts as first dc), (2dc) in same st as first ch3, ch2, *sk2 sc, (3dc) in next st, ch2; rep from * 8 times more, sl st to top of first ch3 to join—10 3dc-groups.

Round 5
ch3 (counts as first dc), dc in same st as first ch3, dc, (2dc) in next stitch, ch2, *sk ch-sp, (2dc) in next st, dc, (2dc) in next st, ch2; rep from * 8 times more, sl st to top of first ch3 to join—10 ch2-sps.

Round 6
ch3 (counts as first dc), dc in same st as first ch3, 3dc, (2dc) in next st, ch2, sk ch-sp, *(2dc) in next st, 3dc, (2dc) in next st, ch2, sk ch-sp; rep from * 8 times more, sl st to top of first ch3 to join.

Round 7
dc-dec by joining first ch3 (counts as first dc) and dc together, 3dc, dc-dec, *ch2, dc in ch-sp, ch2, dc-dec, 3dc, dc-dec; rep from * 8 times more, ch2, dc in ch-sp, ch2, sl st to top of first dc-dec to join—20 ch2-sps.

Round 8
dc-dec by joining first ch3 (counts as first dc) and dc together, dc, dc-dec, ch3, dc in next ch-sp, ch3, dc in next ch-sp, ch3, *dc-dec, dc, dc-dec, ch3, dc in next ch-sp, ch3, dc in next ch-sp, ch3; rep from * 8 times more, sl st to top of first dc-dec to join—50dc.

Round 9
d-dc-dec by joining first ch3 (counts as first dc) and 2dc together, ch3, dc in ch-sp, ch3, dc in next ch-sp, ch3, dc in next ch-sp, ch3, *d-dc-dec, ch3, dc in ch-sp, ch3, dc in next ch-sp, ch3, dc in next ch-sp, ch3; rep from * 8 times more, sl st to top of first d-dc-dec to join—40dc.

Round 10
ch2 (counts as first sc), sc in ch-sp, sc in next dc, (2sc) in next ch-sp, sc in next dc, sc in next ch-sp, sc in next dc, (2sc) in next ch-sp, *sc in top of next d-dc-dec, sc in next ch-sp, sc in next dc, (2sc) in next ch-sp, sc in next dc, sc in next ch-sp, sc in next dc, (2sc) in next ch-sp; rep from * 8 times more, sl st to top of first ch2 to join—100sc.

Round 11
ch3 (counts as first dc), dc in each st around, sl st to top of first ch3 to join—100 dc.

Round 12
ch3 (counts as first dc), dc in same stitch, 4dc, *(2dc) in next st, 4dc; rep from * 18 times more, sl st to top of first ch3 to join—120dc.

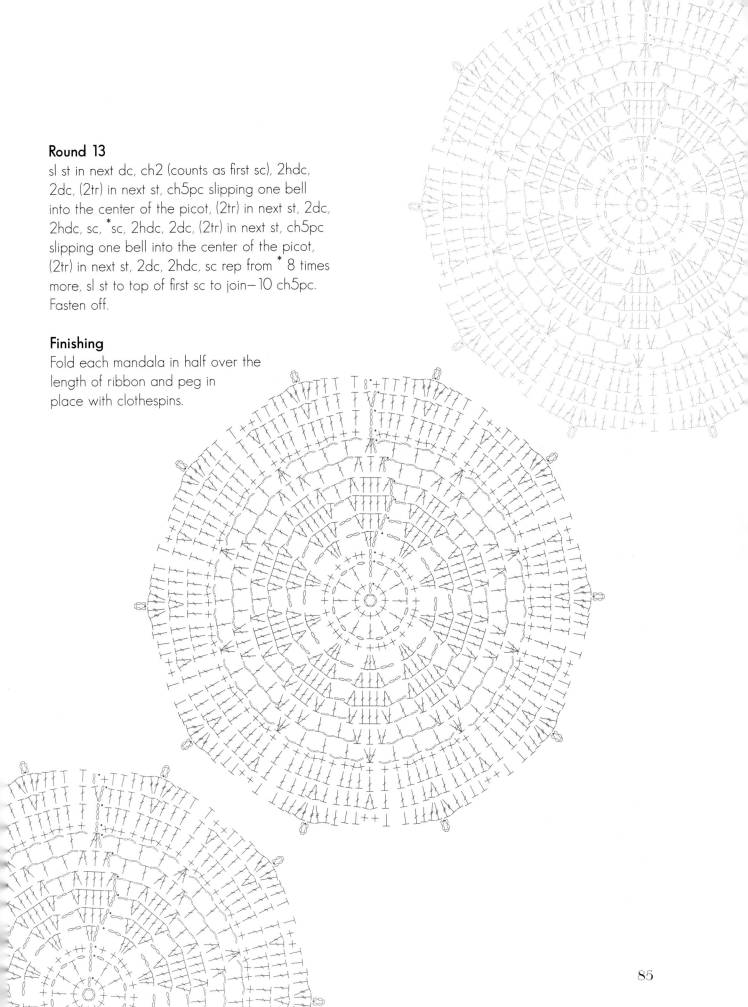

Round 13

sl st in next dc, ch2 (counts as first sc), 2hdc, 2dc, (2tr) in next st, ch5pc slipping one bell into the center of the picot, (2tr) in next st, 2dc, 2hdc, sc, *sc, 2hdc, 2dc, (2tr) in next st, ch5pc slipping one bell into the center of the picot, (2tr) in next st, 2dc, 2hdc, sc rep from * 8 times more, sl st to top of first sc to join—10 ch5pc. Fasten off.

Finishing

Fold each mandala in half over the length of ribbon and peg in place with clothespins.

SUMMER SOLSTICE SUNRISE BLANKET

A stunning, attention grabbing blanket worked in a sumptuous wool/cotton blend. The uniform frame color anchors the color palette and proves a delicate base for the stunning ombrè of color within the motifs.

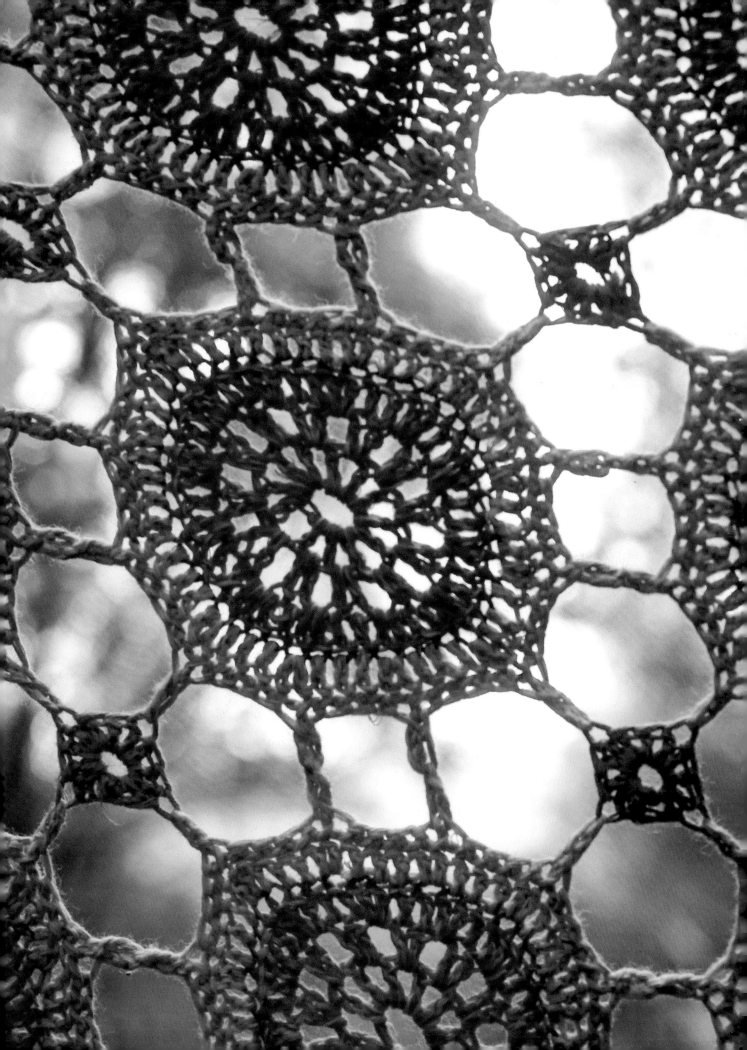

SUMMER SOLSTICE SUNRISE BLANKET

Designed by Anita Mundt

Sample measures 53in. x 67in. (135cm x 170cm)
Each circle measures approximately 4½ in./12 cm.

Materials

- 2 x 900m balls each of Wol Café Unikat 'Limited By' cotton/wool color: 0027 (A) and 0031 (B)
- 1 x 900m balls of Wol Café Unikat 'Limited By cotton/wool color: Deep Turquoise (C)
- Crochet hook size C-2 (2.75mm)

Note: The blanket is worked diagonally, from corner to corner, joining the circles as you go.

Chart does not show beginning and end of rounds. See written instructions.

Stitches & Abbreviations

ch: chain

ch5pc (picot using 5 chain stitches): ch5, sl st in first ch to form picot

ch-sp(s): chain space(s)

dc: double crochet

dc-bl: double crochet into back loop only

rep: repeat

sc: single crochet

sl st: slip stitch

st(s): stitch(es)

*: work following sequence of stitches; repeat sequence designated number of times more

( ): stitches between parentheses to be worked into the same stitch or space

CIRCLE (make 192)

CIRCLE CENTER

With A, ch6, sl st to first ch to form a ring.

Round 1

ch4 (counts as first dc, ch1), *dc in ring, ch1; rep from * 10 times more, sl st to top of first ch3 to join—12dc.

Round 2

ch3 (acts as first dc), dc in same dc, ch1, *(2dc) in next dc, ch1; rep from * 10 times more, sl st to top of first ch3 to join—24dc.

Round 3

ch3 (counts as first dc), dc, (2dc) in next ch-sp, *2dc, (2dc) in next ch-sp; rep from * 10 times more, changing to B in last dc, sl st to back loop only of the top of first ch3 to join—48dc. Cut A.

CIRCLE OUTER

Join the circles through the picots as shown on chart.

Round 4

With B, ch3 (counts as first dc), 2dc-bl, (2dc-bl) in next dc, *3dc-bl, (2dc-bl) in next dc; rep from * 10 times more, sl st to top of first ch3 to join.

Round 5

ch2 (counts as first sc), 4sc, ch5pc, *5sc, ch5pc; rep from * 10 times more, sl st to top of first ch2 to join. Fasten off.

JOINING

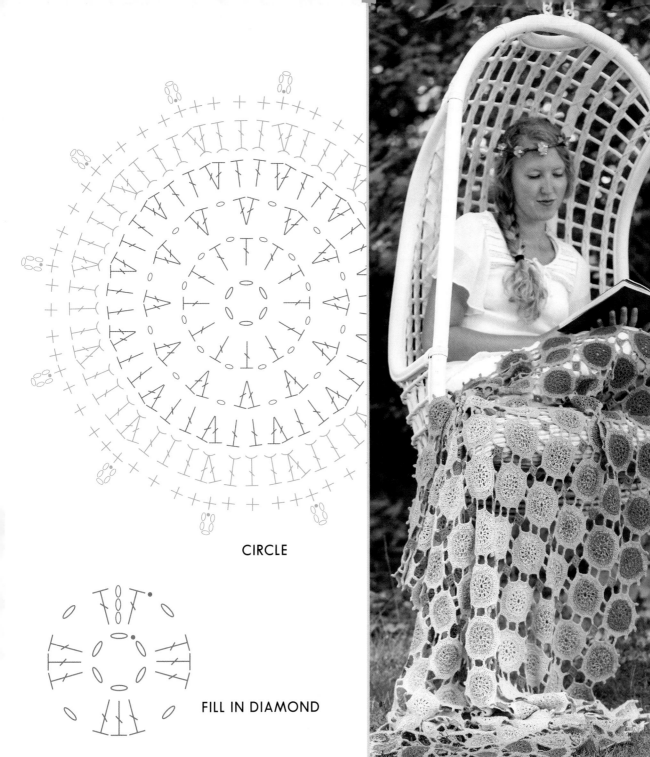

CIRCLE

FILL IN DIAMOND

FILL IN DIAMONDS

The chain stitches in round 2 join to the outer circles as shown on the diagram.

ch6, sl st to first ch to form ring.

Round 1

ch3 (counts as first dc), dc in ring, ch1, *3dc in ring, ch1; rep from * twice more, dc in ring, sl st to top of first ch3 to join. Fasten off.

STARLIGHT STOOL COVER

Upholstry can change your furniture, and this simple crocheted version can be worked up in an afternoon. The addition of satin ribbon at the bottom allows you to easily adjust the cover to fit your stool.

Designed by Anita Mundt

To cover a stool top 14in. (36cm) in diameter

Materials

- Crochet hook size K-10.5 (6.5mm)
- 1 skein of WoolWench Hand Painted Superwash Yarn in Pine
- Satin ribbon 1.5m/1.5yd long
- Sewing needle and thread

Stitches & Abbreviations

ch: chain

dc: double crochet

dc-cl: dc cluster made with 4 dc stitches by working 4dc in same st to the last yo and drawing final yo of final dc through all rem loops on hook

rep: repeat

sc: single crochet

sk: skip

sl st: slip stitch

st: stitch

yo: yarn over

*: work following sequence of stitches; repeat sequence designated number of times more

( ): stitches between parentheses to be worked into the same stitch or space

[ ]: repeat sequence of stitches between brackets designated number of times

Note

Chart does not show beginning and end of rounds. See written instructions.

STOOL COVER

ch5, join with sl st to first ch to form ring.

Round 1

ch2 (counts as first sc), 9sc in ring, sl st to top of first ch2 to join—10sc.

Round 2

ch3 (counts as first dc), *(2dc) in next st; rep from * 8 times more, dc in same stitch as starting ch3, sl st to top of starting ch3 to join—20sc.

Round 3

dc-cl (using ch3 as first dc), ch1, *dc-cl, ch1 rep from * 18 times more, sl st to top of first ch3 to join—20dc-cl.

Round 4

sl st in next ch-sp, dc-cl (using ch3 as first dc), ch2, *(dc-cl in next ch-sp, ch2); rep from * 18 times more, sl st to top of first ch3 to join—20dc-cl.

Round 5

dc-cl (using ch3 as first dc), ch1, [dc-cl in next ch-sp, ch1, dc-cl in next dc-cl, ch1] twice, dc-cl in next ch-sp, ch2, *sk dc-cl, [dc-cl in next ch-sp, ch1, dc-cl in next dc-cl, ch1] 3 times, dc-cl in next ch-sp, ch2; rep from * 3 times, sk dc-cl, dc-cl in next ch-sp, ch1, sl sl to top of first dc-cl to join—35dc-cl.

Round 6

sl st in ch-sp, dc-cl (using ch3 as first dc), ch1, [dc-cl in next ch-sp, ch1] 3 times, dc-cl in next ch-sp, ch5, (sk dc-cl, ch-sp, dc-cl), *[dc-cl in next ch-sp, ch1] 5 times, dc-cl in next ch-sp, ch 5, (sk dc-cl, ch-sp, dc-cl); repeat from * 3 times, dc-cl in next ch-sp, ch1, sl st to top of first dc-cl to join—30dc-cl.

Round 7

sl st in ch-sp, dc-cl (using ch3 as first dc), ch1, [dc-cl in next ch-sp, ch1] twice, dc-cl in next ch-sp, ch9, (sk dc-cl, ch-sp, dc-cl), *[dc-cl in next ch-sp, ch1] 4 times, dc-cl in next ch-sp, ch 9, (sk dc-cl, ch-sp, dc-cl); repeat from * 3 times, dc-cl in next ch-sp, ch1, sl st to top of first dc-cl to join—25dc-cl.

Round 8

sl st in ch-sp, dc-cl (using ch3 as first dc), ch1, dc-cl in next ch-sp, ch1, dc-cl in next ch-sp, ch15, (sk dc-cl, ch-sp, dc-cl), *[dc-cl in next ch-sp, ch1] 3 times, dc-cl in next ch-sp, ch 15, (sk dc-cl, ch-sp, dc-cl); repeat from * 3 times, dc-cl in next ch-sp, ch1, sl st to top of first dc-cl to join—20dc-cl.

Round 9

sl st in ch-sp, dc-cl (using ch3 as first dc), ch1, dc-cl in next ch-sp, ch19, (sk dc-cl, ch-sp, dc-cl), *[dc-cl in next ch-sp, ch1] twice, dc-cl in next ch-sp, ch 19, (sk dc-cl, ch-sp, dc-cl); repeat from * 3 times, dc-cl in next ch-sp, ch1, sl st to top of first dc-cl to join—15dc-cl.

Round 10

sl st in ch-sp, dc-cl (using ch3 as first dc), ch8, sc in ch19-sp, ch8, *dc-cl in next ch-sp, ch1, dc-cl in next ch-sp, ch 8, sc in ch19-sp, ch 8; rep from * 3 times, dc-cl in next ch-sp, ch1, sl st to top of first dc-cl to join—10dc-cl.

Round 11

ch3 (counts as first dc, 8dc in ch8-sp, dc in sc, 8dc in ch8-sp, *dc in dc-cl, dc in ch1-sp, dc in dc-cl, 8dc in ch8-sp, dc in sc, 8dc in ch8-sp; rep from * 3 times, dc in dc-cl, dc in ch1-sp, sl st to top of first dc to join—100dc.

Rounds 12—14 (not shown on chart)

ch3 (counts as dc), dc in each st around, sl st to top of first ch3 to join. Fasten off. Sew satin ribbon to the edge of the stool cover leaving enough ribbon to tie a bow at each end.

CHART SYMBOLS

⌒ chain (ch)

• slip stitch (sl st)

+ single crochet (sc)

T half double crochet (hdc)

T double crochet (dc)

T treble crochet (tr)

T double treble crochet (dt)

⌒ through back loop (BLO)

⌣ through front loop (FLO)

T front post double crochet (fpdc)

V double crochet increase (dc-inc)

A double crochet decrease (dc-dec)

A double dc decrease (d-dc-dec)

⬚ double crochet cluster (dc-cl)

⬚ popcorn stitch (dc5pop)

◊ puff stitch (pf) or double crochet cluster (dc-cl)

◊◊ puff stitch decrease (pf2tog)

picot (pc)

chain-5 picot (ch5pc)

chain-7 picot (ch7pc)